LUTHER ON JUSTIFICATION

D1572551

LUTHER
ON
JUSTIFICATION

Robin A. Leaver

Publishing House
St. Louis

2 3 4 5 6 7 8 9 10 11 WP 89 88 87 86 85 84 83 82 81 80

Concordia Publishing House, St. Louis, Missouri

Copyright © 1975 Concordia Publishing House

MANUFACTURED IN THE UNITED STATES OF AMERICA

Library of Congress Cataloging in Publication Data

Leaver, Robin A
    Luther on justification.

    Includes bibliographical references.
    1. Justification — History of doctrines.
2. Luther, Martin, 1483-1546 — Theology. I. Title.
BR333.5.J8L4 1975   234'.7'0924   74-17035

Preface

Robin A. Leaver's *Luther on Justification* is a most useful hand-book and will be to many a sound introduction to the core and heart of Luther's doctrine of salvation. It is a chief merit of the work that it is content to put little signposts along the way, but that in the main the work consists of many hundreds of fine quotations from Luther himself. Luther himself, unlike the theologians who comment on him, was a rather simple person, and what he has to say comes out always directly, and quite often beautifully, so that anybody coming to the study of Luther at Leaver's hands will get something of the flavor not only of Luther's doctrine but of the great Reformer himself.

Of course, what the author gives us is still only a tiny selection of the many thousands of places where Luther discusses these things. The footnotes indicate where the major references may be found, and there will no doubt be many readers who will turn from these citations to such treatises as the *Sermon on Good Works, The Liberty of a Christian Man, Against Latomus,* the *Theses Concerning Justification,* and the last great commentary upon Genesis, as they are now available for English-speaking readers in the American edition.

Luther was misunderstood about these things within the Roman church almost universally until our own time. The notion that he thought of faith as intellectual belief alone, that he thought of faith isolated, on the one hand, from faith's object: God in Jesus Christ and from the fruits of faith, that is, from in works of faith and love — these notions, the very notions against which he fought so vehemently the scholastic theologians and the

5

antinomians within his own ranks, are at least well and truly nailed down in this little book. The numerous quotations given are admirably footnoted in modern secondary studies. The author is to be congratulated in subtracting this one theme, and amply documenting it, from the vast complex of modern Reformation studies and research into Martin Luther. The wayfaring Christian who needs to know what Luther taught about the heart of the Gospel, and who wants to know it in Luther's own words, will find ample satisfaction in these pages.

Those who have the time, the equipment, and indeed the vocation to go deeper and further will find this an admirable introduction, opening the way out into the beginning of what could well be a lifetime's research and study, as some of us could testify, of an infinitely enriching and worthwhile kind.

Cambridge, England   GORDON RUPP

Contents

Chapter One

Justification

It is a commonplace to say that Martin Luther rediscovered the doctrine of justification by faith alone. It has been said many times; this is his heritage. And yet when one examines his tremendous literary output, it is surprising to find that there is not one work completely devoted to a full-scale presentation of this doctrine he reopened for us.

Now this does not mean that it was not his intention to do so. On the contrary, in his open letter *On Translating* (1530), after explaining why he added the word "alone" in his translation of Romans 3:28,[1] he writes: "Let this be enough for the present. If God gives me grace, I shall have more to say about it in the tract 'On Justification.' "[2]

This work was never completed, although there are in existence a few fragments in the form of notes and outlines from which he obviously intended to write the work.[3] But nothing full-scale appeared.

An Advantage

Some would reckon that this is a distinct disadvantage, because it means that we have to hunt through his many writings to see what his doctrine really is. In fact, this is an advantage. If Luther had written this one work on justification, it would have been taken as his last word on the subject, and what he had said elsewhere would have been ignored. This would have been a great loss, for it is inconceivable, even for Luther, that he should be able to compress the richness of the varied ways in which he explains this fundamental of the faith, scattered throughout his writings, into just one small volume. As it is, Luther has forced us to consult his writings extensively and intensively.

As we begin ferreting through his works to understand his mind on justification, we are immediately presented with a serious problem. It was the Roman Catholic Church that gave birth to Luther. He was well and truly cast in the Roman Catholic mold. Now, because of this, it means that his thought-forms, certainly at the beginning of his career, as we would expect, are conditioned by this background.

When Luther discovered justification,[4] he was still a Roman Catholic; therefore, when he came to explain this experience and this insight, he inevitably used the technical language of scholastic theology. The problem is simply this: Is Luther advocating a new doctrine or a refurbishing of the old one?

The answer will be particularly important for evaluating Luther's doctrine during his earlier years, while he was still within the Catholic fold. In other words, did his doctrine of justification develop?

Divergent View

Many Catholics are of the opinion that Luther's doctrine retains the Catholic sense. "Luther," writes J. M. Todd, "was propounding a radically new presentation of theology . . . and he was doing it as a good Catholic." [5] Some have gone so far as to state that only Melanchthon's doctrine of justification was condemned by the Council of Trent and not Luther's.[6]

On the other hand, there are those Protestants who insist that Luther's doctrine is considerably different from traditional Catholicism. "His doctrine of justification," writes Werner Elert, "is not a mere variation of the medieval doctrine; it ushers in a new epoch." [7] It is Heinrich Böhmer's recurring theme that Luther was pouring new wine into old bottles.[8]

With this divergence of views concerning Luther's doctrine we must be extremely careful to see exactly what he means as we read him. After all, this is what he himself requested: "But above all else, I beg the sincere reader, and I beg for the sake of our Lord Jesus Christ Himself, to read those things judiciously.

10

May he be mindful of the fact that I was once a monk and a most enthusiastic papist when I began that cuase." [9]

Date of Discovery

Luther discovered justification in the verse Romans 1:17. Looking back on it in later life, he writes: "Though I lived as a monk without reproach,[10] I felt that I was a sinner before God with an extremely disturbed conscience. I could not believe that He was placated by my satisfaction. . . . At last, by the mercy of God, meditating day and night, I gave heed to the context of the words, namely, 'In it the righteousness of God is revealed, as it is written, "He who through faith is righteous shall live." ' Here I felt that I was altogether born again and had entered Paradise itself through open gates." [11]

Traditionally this formative experience has been assigned to the year 1519—that is, after his important early lectures on Psalms, Romans, Hebrews, and Galatians, and 2 years after the indulgence skirmish. But since the beginning of this century the tendency has been to assign this experience to an earlier date.

E. Gordon Rupp maintains "it is clear, in all essentials, [that] his theology was in existence before the opening of the Church struggle in 1517." [12] Roland Bainton also seems to suggest this period of 1516-1517.[13] Even more radical is Heinrich Böhmer, who maintains that Luther's discovery took place in April or May 1513, that is, before his first lectures on the Psalms.[14]

Most writers lean toward this earlier date, with the exception of a few, among them Uuvas Saarnivaara, who argues that Luther's discovery took place as late as the winter of 1518-1519.[15]

Certainly it must have taken place before 1517. The spring of that year saw Luther's first publication, an interpretation and translation of *The Seven Penitential Psalms*.[16] In this work Luther clearly distinguishes the complete difference between man's righteousness and God's righteousness [17] and anticipates his famous sermon *On Two Kinds of Righteousness* of 1519.[18]

"The ultimate implication of this interpretation of divine justice is that man is expected to attribute his justification to God without any reservation whatever. God is seen in a double role. He is first of all the supreme authority that demands justice from man . . . and secondly, He is the fulfiller of His own demand . . . He who *requires* perfect justice also *gives* it." [19]

The implication of Bluhm's thesis is that Luther must have discovered justification before the spring of 1517, because by that time "Luther was quite ready to communicate to the man in the street at least something of what was, as well as he knew by that time, a major departure from the then prevailing views." [20]

Mystic Theology and Scholastic Theology

Sometime during 1516 Luther came across the sermons of the mystic Johann Tauler (d. 1361) and the small theological booklet to which he gave the name *A German Theology*. In both these works there is a single theme: Suffer God, for everything depends on it. By this the mystics meant the rigorous self-discipline which is the necessary preparation for the union of the soul with God.[21]

Luther read this theme of "suffer God," but unlike the mystics he was thinking of justification—the free gift of God. "Thus Luther always read his own thoughts into the two mystics. He reinterpreted the whole mystical terminology and gave it his own meaning, as can be seen especially in the second course of lectures on the Psalms (1518)." [22]

And what can be said of Luther's attitude toward these mystics can also be said of his attitude toward scholastic theology: he uses traditional language to express something different, scholastic vocabulary to convey Luther-an theology. "Man, like a plant, takes from his environment only what agrees with his nature." [23]

For an example of this working in the opposite direction, during 1966 loyal, devout Roman Catholics in Venice lobbied the Vatican's weekly *Osservatore Della Domenica* for the canonization of the composer Johann Sebastian Bach—a staunch Lutheran in his day, whose music expresses distinctive Lutheran theology! But these Catholics saw in Bach's music only that which agreed with their theological presuppositions.[24]

I quote Böhmer again: "Luther was offering new wine in old

bottles. This at once becomes clear when one asks what faith is. Faith, wrote Luther, is not a work of man. It is a disposition produced by God, or, more correctly, the consciousness of new life which takes root in the soul when it has gained the assurance of God's favor through the glad tidings of God's love in Christ. . . .

"Thus the prevailing Catholic view was simply reversed by Luther. What one does to win God's favor—as fasting, telling one's beads, making pilgrimages, endowing masses, building churches and monasteries—is not good, but that is good which God Himself does indirectly in and through man, by means of the consciousness of new life brought about by faith which He has awakened." [25]

Therefore it seems that Luther certainly made his discovery of justification before 1516,[26] and possibly even earlier. And, as he says himself, this discovery was decisive.

Personal Problem

It was not that Luther was first upset by abuses in the church and as he began to tackle them discovered the Gospel. No. At the beginning it was a personal problem expressed in the Biblical question: "What must I do to be saved?" and not until Luther received the Biblical answer: "Believe on the Lord Jesus Christ" [27] did he go on to tackle church problems.

From the time of this experience—whenever it was—the doctrine of justification by faith alone became his controlling principle.[28] It was not that his doctrine changed over the years; it was Luther who changed. He began to see bit by bit the implications of justification by faith alone which eventually led him outside the ranks of the Roman Catholic Church.

Toward the end of his life he wrote: "Twenty years ago I taught—as I still do—that faith alone, without works, justifies. But if someone had arisen at that time and taught that monkery and nunning ought to be called idolatry and the mass a veritable abomination, I, though I would not have helped to burn him, would at least have said that it served him right. And I—thoughtless fool—could not see the conclusion that I would have had to concede that if faith alone does it, then monkery and mass do not." [29]

But Luther consistently advised his fellow evangelicals to introduce the Reformation slowly, beginning with the doctrine of justification. When this is in its rightful place, it will transform everything else, and this Luther knew from experience.

Manner of Reform

In the letter to the clergy of Lübeck, January 12, 1530, he wrote: "We . . . request and exhort you with godly solicitude that you do not begin with innovations in rites, which are dangerous, but that you undertake such changes later. Put first and foremost what is fundamental in our teaching, the doctrine concerning our justification; namely, that we are justified by another's righteousness, even Christ's, which is given to us in faith and which by God's grace is apprehended by those who are first terrified by the law and who, struck by the consciousness of their sins, sigh for redemption.

"It does not help to talk to others of God's grace, for they will perceive only the external change in rites, which will tickle their fancy for an hour or so but will in time cause them to be sated and to loathe all sound doctrine. Reform of impious rites will come by itself when what is fundamental in our teaching, being effectively presented, has taken root in pious hearts.

"Such people will at once recognize how great an abomination and how sacrilegious a blasphemy that papistic idolatry (namely, the Mass and other abuses of the Sacrament) is, and so it is unnecessary to fish in front of the net; that is, to demolish the traditions before the righteousness of faith is understood." [30]

A Caution

Luther's was a different theology. Yet, as we have seen, although the content was new, the vocabulary was old, and Luther was well aware of this. "Every theologian," he said, "ought to speak according to a certain pattern. . . . In fact, we have to speak in this way on account of the teaching of the sophists, for one must stammer with the stammerers." [31]

14

Luther was conditioned by his environment, a fact that made it easy for his contemporaries to understand him, a fact that makes it easy for us to misunderstand him. Therefore we shall need to take care to be sure that we have grasped exactly what Luther meant.

Chapter Two

Sola

In the year 1517 Luther came out into the open in the affair concerning indulgences. He complained about the fact that his parishioners in Wittenberg could go and buy certificates of justification made out in their own name or in the name of a deceased loved one.

In the eyes of the people, the church was seen to be offering them eternal insurance policies, and, provided that the premium was fully paid, the benefits were guaranteed. "The certificate therefore represented a title deed to salvation, visible to the eye and absolutely sure if correctly used." [1]

Aftermath to Indulgences

This confronted Luther with a difficult pastoral problem, for what man, possessing one such certificate in his own name, would be interested in churchgoing, hearing sermons, attending the sacraments, or living according to Christian standards? Such a man would put his trust in his piece of paper: whatever his conduct and belief, his eternal future was secure, and he had it in writing to prove it.

This situation brought forth from Luther his now famous *Ninety-Five Theses Concerning Indulgences*, [2] in which he stresses the need for continual repentance in the Christian life and that the Christian's trust is not in any piece of paper but in the person of the Lord Jesus Christ. The facts of Luther's intervention and the content of these Theses spread very quickly throughout Germany, and, important though it was, this whole affair was but the noisy prelude to the great drama of the con-

16

tinuing controversy between himself and the Roman Catholic Church.

The root of this controversy is to be found in a four-letter word — *sola,* alone. For Luther it was justification by faith alone — *sola.*

It was not that justification was a new doctrine, for it had always had a definite place within the framework of medieval scholastic theology. In this it was held that by some means God's grace and man's free will work together in man's salvation. Justification is a distinct stage in the upward movement of man toward God.

Catholic View of Justification

For Thomas Aquinas justification was merely one question among many others.[3] And this is the traditional Catholic view of justification, that it is, together with regeneration, predestination, sanctification, and so on, one of the many facets of the event of Jesus Christ.

Hans Küng, a contemporary Catholic theologian, can write: "Justification is not the central dogma of Christianity. . . . The central *dogma* of *Christianity* is the mystery of Christ."[4]

For traditional Catholicism the question of justification is "as well as"; for Luther it is "either or."[5] In traditional Catholicism it is an absurd one-sidedness for justification to be considered as occurring through faith alone. For Luther it was equally absurd not to talk of justification by faith alone. And here are the seeds of the controversy.

After ominous rumblings and a few violent outbursts, the justification storm finally broke in 1522 when Luther published his German translation of the New Testament. The rock of offense was his translation of Romans 3:28, into which he introduces the word "alone," so that the verse reads: "For we hold that a man is justified by faith *alone* apart from works of the Law."

Sola Against Tradition

This brought forth the wrath of his opponents, notably Jerome Emser,[6] theologian and secretary to Duke George of

Saxony. The opposition to Luther's translation was bitter and violent. Without the little four-letter word *sola* any statement from Luther or his followers could be interpreted in the traditional Catholic way, and they were continually under pressure to drop it.

At the Diet of Augsburg in 1530 Luther's old opponent Eck tried to get Melanchthon to drop the word. Melanchthon wrote to Luther: "Eck finds fault with the word *sola*. He does not condemn the doctrine itself but says that the unlearned would be offended by it. I forced him to admit that we are right in ascribing righteousness to faith." [7]

Luther replied: "You write that you made Eck admit that we are justified by faith. If only you had persuaded him not to lie!" [8]

The verbal formula may have been identical, but what Eck meant by justification and what Luther meant by it were two different things.

During the same year, 1530, Luther wrote his open letter *On Translating*.[9] It was probably written more for the enlightenment of his friends than for the confounding of his enemies.[10] Luther says that it was a letter to answer two questions that a "friend" had asked him, but it may well have been simply a literary device [11] to air two doctrinal issues: justification by faith alone and the question of the intercession of the saints.

The fact that the second question is treated so cursorily makes it clear that Luther wanted his readers to fasten their attention on the doctrine of justification. He does this by talking about the art of translating Biblical Greek into contemporary German, and he uses five texts to illustrate his principles.

But it is Romans 3:28 which is the center of it all. He devotes twice as much space to the consideration of this verse than all the other verses put together. "It is Romans 3:28 around which the essay really revolves, no matter how interesting and exciting the other verses may be and actually are in their own right." [12]

Luther's Defense of *Sola*

The controversy centered around this four-letter word — *sola* (although in this particular instance, to be grammatically correct, it ought to be *solum,* as Luther points out [13]). His opponents criticized him for adding the word to the Biblical text. Their argument was that as the word, or its equivalent, is not there in the Greek, so it should be absent from the German translation.

Luther replies: "Here in Romans 3[:28] I know very well that the word *solum* is not in the Greek or Latin text; the papists do not have to teach me that. It is a fact that these four letters *s o l a* are not there. And these blockheads stare at them like cows at a new gate. At the same time they do not see that it conveys the sense of the text; it belongs there if the translation is to be clear and vigorous. I wanted to speak German, not Latin or Greek, since it was German I had undertaken to speak in translation." [14]

And this is his continuing argument.

Although *sola* is not absolutely necessary in this verse, its use makes the phrase "without works of the law" abundantly clear. Luther was not translating for the scholastic mind, which had a ready access to the New Testament in Latin or Greek; he was translating for the man in the street, and he wanted his translation to be as clear and as unambiguous as possible.

"I inserted the word *solum* (alone) [into Romans 3:28]. Actually the text itself and the meaning of St. Paul urgently require and demand it. For in that passage he is dealing with the main point of Christian doctrine; namely, that we are justified by faith in Christ without any works of the law. And Paul cuts away all works so completely, as even to say that the works of the law—though it is God's law and Word—do not help for justification. . . . " [15]

"But when all works are so completely cut away—and that must mean that faith alone justifies—whoever would speak plainly and clearly about this cutting away of works will have to say, 'Faith alone justifies us, and not works.' The matter itself, as well as the nature of the language, demand it." [16]

Thomas Aquinas' *Sola*

Luther insists that there is nothing novel in *sola fide,* and he points out that St. Augustine, St. Ambrose, and many others had understood St. Paul in the same way.[17] Perhaps Luther included Thomas Aquinas in the "many others"!

Joseph Lortz, the foremost Roman Catholic Reformation scholar, has pointed out that the Angelic Doctor also maintained that the ultimate meaning of St. Paul is *sola fide*.[18] But, as we might expect, there is a considerable difference between what Aquinas meant by justification and what Luther meant by it, even though they may use the same vocabulary—*sola fide*.

As we have already seen, justification for Aquinas is simply one question among many others; for Luther it is the one fundamental theological question. In the passage from the open letter *On Translating* quoted above, in which Luther explains his rendering of Romans 3:28, it becomes clear that his use of the word *sola* is far more radical than just a striking translation of the verse.

Not only is it *fide* which is *sola*—the doctrine of justification itself is *sola*. For Luther it is, to quote him again, "the main point of Christian doctrine." [19] For Aquinas the doctrine of justification is *also*—part of the general theme of man's ascent to God. For Luther it is *sola*—it stands by itself; it is the new relationship between the sinner and God through Jesus Christ.

Importance of Justification

In a multitude of metaphors Luther explains the importance of the doctrine of justification. It is "the proposition of primary importance" [20] because "Christ wants us to concentrate our attention on this chief doctrine, our justification before God, in order that we may believe in Him." [21] It is "the cardinal doctrine of justification by faith in Christ," [22] "the true and chief article of Christian doctrine." [23]

"This doctrine is the chief intention of the book [of the Acts of the Apostles] and the author's principal reason for writing it." [24] Justification is "the pure doctrine of faith" [25] and the "one doctrine of Christian righteousness." [26]

"This article is the head and cornerstone which alone begets, nourishes, builds, preserves, and protects the church; without it the church of God cannot subsist one hour." [27]

"On this article rests all that we teach and practice against the pope, the devil, and the world." [28]

The doctrine of justification is, in its Latin formula, *articulus stantis vel cadentis ecclesiae* — the article of faith that decides whether a church is standing or falling, or as J. I. Packer explains it: "For the doctrine of justification is like Atlas: it bears a world on its shoulders, the entire evangelical knowledge of saving grace. . . . When Atlas falls, everything that rested on his shoulders comes crashing down too." [29]

Luther never tires of explaining that where the doctrine of justification by faith is understood, there the spiritual life of the church is really alive in Jesus Christ; but where justification is unknown, there is no spiritual life at all.

"A token or a painted gulden is not the real thing; it is only a representation. In fact, it is worthless and a fraud if it is given or considered as a real gulden, while a genuine gulden is such in truth and without deception. So the life, work, and righteousness of the conceited saints is, in comparison with the righteousness and work of the grace of God, only a semblance and a deadly, harmful fraud if it is held to be the real thing. This is not the truth, but the real truth is that of God, who gives the genuine and fundamental righteousness, namely, faith in Christ." [30]

Purity of Doctrine Essential

This doctrine of justification can never be abandoned or adulterated: "Nothing in this article can be given up or compromised, nor can any believer concede or permit anything contrary to it, even if heaven and earth and things temporal should be destroyed. . . . On this article rests all that we teach and practice against the pope, the devil, and the world. Therefore we must be quite certain and have no doubts about it. Otherwise all is lost, and the pope, the devil, and all our adversaries will gain the victory." [31]

And again: "Where this single article remains pure, Christendom will remain pure, in beautiful harmony, and without any schisms. But where it does not remain pure, it is impossible to repel any error or heretical spirit." [32]

21

One such error, and a common one at that, is spiritual simony. "One can see how pitiable and dangerous a matter it is to have fallen away from the proposition of primary importance – the proposition concerning justification by faith without works. When it has become obscured and obliterated, the entire world becomes addicted to simony [33] . . . to buy spiritual things for money and merits. Therefore it is simony by name, like that described in canon law. . . . every human being is a simonist by nature and would want God to be so constituted that He would be appeased by human works and merits." [34]

And the substance of this spiritual simony is idolatry: where the doctrine of justification is known and understood, there is true worship; without it there can be only the worship of false gods – idolatry. "Whoever falls from the doctrine of justification is ignorant of God and is an idolater. . . . For once this doctrine is undermined, nothing more remains but sheer error, hypocrisy, wickedness, and idolatry, regardless of how great the sanctity that appears on the outside." [35]

Justification: Basis of All Doctrines

Luther insists that the doctrine of justification is the kingpin of Christendom. Where it is missing, there can be no true foundation for faith, and men will turn to other doctrines and ideas for their fundamental tenet and will produce a Babel of theologies.

"Therefore I say that there is no force that can resist the sects, and no remedy against them except this one doctrine of Christian righteousness. If this doctrine is lost, it is impossible for us to be able to resist any errors or sects. We can see this today in the fanatics, Anabaptists, and Sacramentarians. Now that they have fallen away from this doctrine, they will never stop falling, erring, and seducing others ad infinitum. Undoubtedly they will arouse innumerable sects." [36]

"Where this knowledge of Christ has disappeared, the sun has lost its light, and there is utter darkness. No article is any longer understood, and one cannot any longer defend himself against any error or false doctrine of the devil.[37] And even though the words regarding faith and Christ are retained, as they are

22

retained in the papacy,[38] the foundation of every single article is lost, and what remains is nothing but foam and uncertain *persuasiones*, or notions, or a painted, feigned faith. . . .

"Where this knowledge has disappeared, everything else has disappeared. You may teach and confess all the articles, as the papists do, but there is no earnest conviction or true understanding of them. It is like groping about in the darkness; it is like a blind man hearing of colors which he has never seen." [39]

For Luther the doctrine of justification by faith alone could never be just one of a series of doctrines. For him it is the one fundamental article of faith on which everything depends. "As I often warn, therefore, the doctrine of justification must be learned diligently. For in it are included all the other doctrines of our faith; if it is sound, all the others are sound as well." [40]

Faith of the Fathers

Luther knows that he is not the first to suggest such a doctrine. His proposition may have been a novelty in his own day, but he maintains that it has always been known somewhere or other. "The faith that we obtain the forgiveness of sins solely for Christ's sake by faith has been the faith of the fathers and the prophets and all saints from the beginning of the world; and it has been the doctrine and teaching of Christ and of the apostles, who were commissioned to spread it in all the world.

"And it is to this day, and will be to the end, the unanimous understanding and voice of the whole Christian church, which always in one mind and with one accord has confessed and fought for this article, that only in the name of Jesus forgiveness of sins is obtained and received. And in this faith they have been justified by God and saved." [41]

Many would feel, perhaps, that Luther has been overzealous in his insistence that this doctrine stands alone, especially in these days when all dogma stands under a cloud of suspicion. As we shall see, Luther is not contending for a mere formula of words but for the new relationship between the sinner and God, which has been made possible by the death of the Lord Jesus Christ. Luther will tenaciously hold on to the doctrine, because

23

if it is overthrown, it would mean that Jesus Christ had been wasting His time on the cross.[42]

Christ *Alone* and Faith *Alone*

"I, Dr. Martinus Luther, unworthy evangelist of our Lord Jesus Christ, I say that this article (faith alone, without any and all works, makes one righteous before God) shall be allowed to stand and to remain. . . . Let that be my, Dr. Luther's, inspiration of the Holy Spirit and the real holy Gospel. For this is the very article which the children pray, 'I believe in Jesus Christ, crucified, dead,' etc.

"No one has died for our sins except *only* Jesus Christ, God's Son—*only* Jesus, God's Son. And once again I say, Jesus, God's Son, *alone,* has redeemed us from sin. That is certainly true and is the whole of Scripture, and even if all the world and the devils tear themselves and burst, it is still true. If, however, it is He *alone* who takes away our sin, then it cannot be with our works.

"It is indeed impossible for me to grasp and attain to this one and *only* Redeemer from sin, Jesus, except through faith. He is and remains beyond the grasp of works. Since faith *alone,* before any works follow it, can lay hold of this Redeemer, so it must be true that *only* faith, before and without works, grasps hold of this redemption, which means nothing else but becoming righteous. For to have been redeemed from sin or to have sin forgiven must be the same as being or becoming righteous, etc.

"Good works, however, follow such faith or redemption or forgiveness of sin or righteousness as the fruit of faith. That is our teaching, as is taught by the Holy Spirit and all of holy Christendom, and with this we remain in God's name. Amen." [43]

Chapter Three

Fide

"Faith is the *conditio sine qua non,* the indispensable condition of theological science, but not its object and theme. How could it ever be its central theme? The real object of theology certainly demands faith, but it also opposes any attempt to dissolve it into thoughts and expressions of faith." So writes Karl Barth.[1]

One of the most persistent criticisms of Luther in particular and of the Protestant Church in general has been that too much emphasis has been placed on man's response of faith. To many, Luther overstated his case, and in his insistence on *sola fide* he in fact advocated a doctrine which he thought he hated! By making justification only possible through *sola fide* Luther had made faith into a work of man, and therefore his doctrine was justification by a work—the work of faith.

Misplaced Stress

In 1838 John Henry Newman complained that "a system of doctrine has risen up during the last 3 centuries in which faith or spiritualmindedness is contemplated and rested on as the end of religion instead of Christ.

"I do not mean to say that Christ is not mentioned as the Author of all good but that stress is laid rather on believing than on the Object of belief, on the comfort and persuasiveness of the doctrine rather than in the doctrine itself.

"And in this way religion is made to consist in contemplating ourselves instead of Christ; not simply in looking to Christ but in *seeing* that we look to Christ, not in His divinity and atonement but in our conversion and faith in them."[2]

Lamentably this caricature has often taken on the form of reality on too many occasions in the history of Protestantism. But whatever we can say concerning such lapses in the history of the church, and indeed in the church of the present day, is this what Luther was advocating—a subjective, introverted experience of emotional willfulness?

One suspects that if Luther had been enabled to read Newman's words, he would have classified them as representing the views of either Anabaptists, sectarians, or fanatics. In his now famous words of his *Preface to the Epistle of St. Paul to the Romans* he himself had protested against such a do-it-yourself faith.

Faith Is God's Activity

"Faith is not the human notion and dream that some people call faith. . . . This is due to the fact that when they hear the Gospel, they get busy and by their own powers create an idea in their heart which says, 'I believe'; they take this then to be a true faith. But, as it is a human figment and idea that never reaches the depths of the heart, nothing comes from it either, and no improvement follows." [3]

When Luther insists on justification *sola fide,* he does not think of faith as something a man does to ensure his salvation. On the contrary, faith for him is the activity of God in the heart of man which produces a new relationship between God and that man. And it all focuses on the person and work of the Lord Jesus Christ.

Luther will often speak of the new relationship between the Christian and Christ in terms of marriage—Christ the Bridegroom, the Christian the bride, and faith as the wedding ring. The wedding ring, the gift of the bridegroom to the bride, is vitally important for a marriage, but its importance is not in itself; it is important for what it does: it brings two people into a new relationship with each other. And so faith is the "token and pledge" of the new relationship between the Christian and Christ.

26

Faith Unites with Christ

Let Luther speak for himself: "Faith . . . unites the soul with Christ as a bride is united with her bridegroom . . . Christ is full of grace, life, and salvation. The soul is full of sins, death, and damnation. Now let faith come between them, and sins, death, and damnation will be Christ's, while grace, life, and salvation will be the soul's, for if Christ is a bridegroom, He must take upon Himself the things which are His bride's and bestow upon her the things that are His. . . .

"Christ is God and man in one person. He has neither sinned nor died, and is not condemned, and he cannot sin, die, or be condemned; His righteousness, life, and salvation are unconquerable, eternal, omnipotent. By the wedding ring of faith [4] he shares in the sins, death, and pains of hell which are His bride's. As a matter of fact, He makes them His own and acts as if they were His own and as if He Himself had sinned; He suffered, died, and descended into hell that He might overcome them all.

"Now since it was such a one who did all this, and death and hell could not swallow Him up, these were necessarily swallowed up by Him in a mighty duel (stupendo duello);[5] for His righteousness is greater than the sins of all men, His life is stronger than death, His salvation more invincible than hell. Thus the believing soul by means of the pledge of its faith is free in Christ, its Bridegroom, free from all sins, secure against death and hell, and is endowed with the eternal righteousness, life, and salvation of Christ its Bridegroom." [6]

Here we have a summary of what Luther meant by faith in justification, which we must now examine in greater detail.

Luther's utterances on faith are legion. His attitude was that as this faith is vital to the Christian's very substance, it must never be forgotten.[7] Therefore, practically every time he opened his mouth to lecture, to preach, or just in conversation, or every time he put his pen to paper, he had something to say about faith. This vast amount of material creates an obvious difficulty in evaluating his thought in the matter, and therefore we shall need some guide.

Theses on Faith

In 1535 Luther prepared his *Theses Concerning Faith and Law*[8] for the doctoral disputation of Hieronymous Weller and Nikolaus Medler. These men were granted their degrees on September 14, 1535, 3 days after the examination, and for this occasion Luther drew up the two sets of theses, one on faith and the other on Law. Luther announces that the underlying theme for all the theses is Romans 3:28: "We hold that a man is justified by faith apart from works of law."[9] There are 71 theses on faith, and we can use them to open up the meaning Luther had for faith.

I

Behind all of Luther's thinking concerning faith there is one basic, negative assumption, and that is that man has no faith and cannot have faith of his own. There is absolutely nothing in man that can work faith in him: his natural powers cannot produce the supernatural gift.

In this Luther parts company with his scholastic background, the theological tradition built on the philosophy of Aristotle, which taught that virtue produces belief, and vice unbelief.[10] For Luther all men without exception are in a state of helpless unbelief.

Unbelief

Thesis 62: "God has consigned all men to unbelief that He may have mercy on all (Romans 11:32). Therefore we are righteous because God is merciful, not because of man's exertion (Romans 9:16)." [11]

This unbelief is the punishment for sin. Ever since the Fall man has been in a state of open rebellion against God. The penalty for such rebellion is the withdrawal of the original freedom that God had given to man, and this has left all men in a slavery to themselves, the slavery of unbelief, which, if it persists, leads to both temporal and eternal death.

Unbelief can never be the no-man's-land between heaven and hell. There are just two simple alternatives, faith or unfaith, and there is no fence to sit on.

28

"In Luther's view," writes Gustav Wingren, "lack of faith is in itself an active thing, for there can be no neutrality between faith and unbelief, between God and the devil. The vacuum, where there is no faith, is filled by unbelief, and that is action against God." [12]

And, of course, this is the main thrust of Luther's great treatise *The Bondage of the Will*.[13] Such is the dilemma of man: he has no faith but needs it desperately. He is hopelessly incapable of obtaining faith for himself but insists on trying to work for it.

"The Scriptures set before us a man who is not only bound, wretched, captive, sick, and dead, but who, through the operation of Satan his lord, adds to his other misdeeds that of blindness, so that he believes himself to be free, happy, possessed of liberty and ability, whole and alive";[14] but "no one can give himself faith, and no more can he take away his own unbelief." [15]

"Historic Faith"

It is because of this state of helpless unbelief that Luther never tires of denouncing "historical faith," [16] that is, an intellectual acceptance of the facts concerning the life, work, and death of Jesus of Nazareth without a personal commitment to that Lord Jesus Christ, the object of faith.

Thesis 2-10: "If Paul is understood to be speaking of acquired or historic faith [in Romans 3:28], he is laboring entirely in vain. . . . if you understand Paul to be speaking of this kind of faith, he is preaching about an idle and fictitious Christ . . . he is necessarily speaking of another kind of faith which shall make Christ effective in us against death, sin, and the law." [17]

"Historic faith" is a "faith" which comes only from the mind, and Luther rejects it because no human mind, however intellectually accomplished, can ever understand what God was doing in Jesus Christ. To the mind the cross was an abysmal failure. The Jewish mind just could not accept a Messiah who was cursed by God, and to the Greek mind the cross was not sophisticated enough to claim its attention.[18]

"Historic faith" sees the facts, acknowledges that they are

true, that they happened, but never gets involved in them. "A counterfeit faith is one that hears about God, Christ, and all the mysteries of the incarnation and redemption, one that also grasps what it hears and can speak beautifully about it; and yet only a mere opinion and a vain hearing remain, which leave nothing in the heart but a hollow sound about the Gospel, concerning which there is a great deal of chatter.

"In fact, this is no faith at all, for it neither renews nor changes the heart. It does not produce a new man but leaves him in his former opinion and way of life. This is a very pernicious faith, and it would be better not to have it. A moral philosopher is better than such a hypocrite with such a faith." [19]

The dichotomy between faith and unbelief is represented by the tension between what God wants to give man and what man wants to get out of God.

True Faith

Theses 20-23: "Acquired faith has as the end or use of Christ's passion mere speculation. True faith has as the end and use of Christ's passion life and salvation. Acquired faith stands like a lazy man concealing his hand under his armpit and says, 'That is nothing to me.' True faith with arms outstretched joyfully embraces the Son of God given for it and says, 'He is my beloved, and I am His.'

"Paul gives an example of this to the Galatians from his own case, saying, 'Who loved me and gave Himself for me' (Galatians 2:20)." [20]

But man always prefers to lay down his conditions on God rather than letting God take over his life absolutely and completely.

"The impure and perverted lovers, who are nothing else than parasites and who seek their own advantage in God, neither love nor praise His bare goodness but have an eye to themselves and consider only how good God is to them. . . . But just as soon as He hides His face and withdraws the rays of His goodness, leaving them bare and in misery, their love and praise are at an end. . . . They delighted in their salvation much more than in their Savior, in the gift more than the Giver, in the creature rather than in the Creator." [21]

True faith will let God be God. Anything else will rob God of everything and put an idol in His place.[22] Faith and God belong together.[23]

There are simply two alternatives which face man: faith or unbelief. Unbelief is his natural condition; faith is the gift of God. Even though a man may talk about faith using the right and proper vocabulary, if it is merely an idea in the head, it is simply not faith; it is unbelief.

"There are two kinds of believing: first a believing about God, which means that I believe that what is said of God is true. This faith is rather a form of knowledge than a faith. There is secondly a believing in God which means that I put my trust in Him, give myself up to thinking I can have dealings with Him, and believe without any doubt that He will be and do to me according to the thing said of Him. Such faith throws itself upon God." [24]

II

Faith is God's answer to man's problem, and it is the only answer. Faith is the gift of God to unbelieving man, and in no way is it to be thought of as a reward. Faith is entirely the gift of God offered to man as the release from his helpless unbelief.

"This treasure is not given as a reward. It is a gift. It is your own. You have only to accept it. It is not a castle but God's Son who is given. Hold out your hand and take." [25]

Faith: God's Gift

From first to last faith is completely the work of God in man. Yes, God demands faith from man, but he is unable to respond to God in this way, and the marvel of faith is that at the same time as God demands faith from man, He, God Himself, also gives it to man.[26] And this is the work of the Holy Spirit in the heart of man.

Thesis 1: "True faith, that gift of the Holy Spirit, must here be understood [in Romans 3:28]." [27] Thesis 15: "Paul preaches this faith, which the Holy Spirit gives and keeps in the hearts of those who hear the voice of the Gospel." [28] And thesis 68: "By the same Spirit we are called righteous, a new creature of God and the first fruits of God's creatures, who according to His will brought us forth by His Word (2 Corinthians 5:17; James 1:18)." [29]

Luther's doctrine of justification by faith alone can only be truly appreciated if his theology of creation is understood. For him creation is *ex nihilo* — out of nothing.

"The Father creates heaven and earth out of nothing through the Son. . . . Over these the Holy Spirit broods. As a hen broods her eggs, keeping them warm in order to hatch her chicks and, as it were, to bring them life through heat, so Scripture says that the Holy Spirit brooded, as it were, on the waters to bring to life those substances which were to be quickened and adorned. For it is the office of the Holy Spirit to make alive." [30]

This is God's creative work — to work through opposites. He creates something from nothing. He brings order and life from chaos and death; from darkness He produces light, and from unbelief He creates faith.[31]

"When God creates faith in man, this is as great a work as if He were to create heaven and earth again." [32] As in God's original creation the creature could not and did not assist the Creator in His bringing it into existence, so in God's re-creation by His Spirit, man is remolded and refashioned without his cooperation: it is entirely the work of God through His Spirit.

"To believe in God is the only true and living faith, which is created within us not by our strength but by God's Spirit." [33]

Faith Changes Man

Faith can never be simply an idea in the head or a mere appreciation of the facts of Jesus Christ. "For faith is a vigorous and powerful thing; it is not idle speculation, nor does it float on the heart like a goose on the water. But just as water that has been heated, even though it remains water, is no longer cold but is hot and an altogether different water, so faith, the work of the Holy Spirit, fashions a different mind and different attitudes and makes us an altogether new human being.

"Therefore faith is an active, difficult, and powerful thing. If we want to consider what it really is, it is something done to us rather than something we do, for it changes the heart and mind." [34]

The original creation was marred by man's sin, that is, man's unilateral declaration of his independence from God, the action which plunged the whole human race into the helpless state of unbelief, which is separation from God. By working faith in man God, so to speak, puts the clock back, recreates that man, and grants to him that freedom which He, God, had intended for man in the first place.

"For the Holy Spirit works faith in us, and through this faith we reign in the image of God we lost in Paradise." [35]

Faith Joins to Christ

As we have already noted, the importance of faith is not in itself but in what it does—it joins the believer to Christ.

"We say that faith is a work of the promise or a gift of the Holy Spirit. Nevertheless faith does not justify in that respect; namely, inasmuch as it is a gift of the Holy Spirit, but inasmuch as it establishes a relation to Christ. For here the principal question is not whence or what sort of work faith is, or in what regard it excels others, since faith does not justify *per se* (on its own account) or by any intrinsic virtue." [36]

This faith is not a patching up of the old creation. It is fundamentally a new work of creation that God performs. By the operation of the Holy Spirit a man is transformed into a totally different person; he is reborn.

Theses 65-67: "Justification is in reality a kind of rebirth in newness, as John says: who believe on His name and were born of God (John 1:12-13; 1 John 5:1)."

After quoting Titus 3:5 and John 3:3 Luther continues: "For that reason it is impossible to be justified by good works, since it is impossible for us to be born of works, but rather the works are born of us, so to speak." [37]

It is for this reason that Luther will reject any suggestion that faith is a sleeping partner, that its presence may be undetected by the person concerned. His argument is that if you have been reborn, you will certainly know about it.[38]

Werner Elert puts it this way: "Through faith the empirical man becomes another person. From a split person he becomes a whole person; from an anguished person, a joyful person; from a person who is not free, a person who is free and 'lord of all things.' "[39]

Faith Brings New Life

Rebirth means an entry into an entirely new existence, a new life, in fact. "Faith acquires Christ's merit and knows that through Christ's death we have been set free. From this source our other righteousness has its origin, namely, that newness of life through which we are zealous to obey God as we are taught by the Word and aided by the Holy Spirit."[40]

This new existence is life in Christ. It is the awareness that the believer lives in Christ, with Christ, through Christ, and for Christ. "Hard on this faith there follows, of itself, a most sweet stirring of the heart whereby the spirit of man is enlarged and enriched (that is love, given by the Holy Spirit through faith in Christ), so that he is drawn to Christ, that gracious and bounteous testator, and made a thoroughly new and different man."[41]

There is no middle ground between faith and unfaith, between no birth and rebirth. New birth is the entry into a new relationship with Christ, and there can be no uncertain hanging around in the doorway,[42] nor can new birth be thought of as an extending, continuing process. It is a single happening.[43]

"This faith makes us joyful and at peace with God, and it must make us love Him, because we see that it is God's will and the gracious attitude of His favor toward us that causes Christ thus to deal with us. This means, then, that we come to the Father and are drawn to the Father through Christ, have peace with God, and unconcernedly and gladly await death and all misfortune. Where such a faith is wanting, there is blindness, there are no Christians, there is not even a spark of God's work and favor."[44]

34

III

God's gift of faith brings about a new awareness of Jesus Christ. It produces a response in man, the personal answer to God's revelation in the Lord Jesus Christ.

Theses 12-14: "This faith, as we put it, apprehends Christ, who died for our sins and rose again for our justification (Romans 4:25). That is, a faith which not only hears the things done by the Jews and Pilate in crucifying Christ or narrated about the resurrection but which understands the love of God the Father, who wants to redeem and save you through Christ, delivered up for your sins." [45]

It is the awareness that what Christ came and did was not to satisfy some idea of His own or that He died for the sins of the world in some vague way. It is the awareness that Christ did everything for me.

Theses 18-19: "True faith says, 'I certainly believe that the Son of God suffered and arose, but He did this all for me, for my sins, of that I am certain. For He died for the sins of the whole world. But it is most certain that I am some part of the world; therefore it is most certain that He died also for me.' " [46]

And again in theses 24-25: "Accordingly, that 'for me' and 'for us,' if it is believed, creates that true faith and distinguishes it from all other faith, which merely hears things done. This is the faith which alone justifies us without law and works through the mercy of God shown in Christ." [47]

Theology of the Word

If the question is asked: On what ground do we know that Christ died for us? Luther will answer, "The Word." "Luther's most central and characteristic thought about faith," writes Paul Althaus, "is that it is born when man is inwardly willing and spiritually convinced by the living voice of God speaking to him in the Word." [48]

The Word for Luther is extremely important, so important in fact that a modern Luther scholar can say that "the theology of Martin Luther was a theology of the Word of God." [49]

This is not the place to make a full investigation into this theology of the Word,[50] but we must appreciate the basic elements. The Word is the living communication from God to men, and it is not simply a synonym for the Bible. The Word is certainly contained in the Bible, but it goes far beyond it and is far greater than the Great Book.

If a man preaches or speaks about God's love in Christ redeeming the world, then that man is a vehicle of the Word. The Word is God's creative activity: God creates by the Word. The Bible has the recurring theme: "God spoke, and it was done. God said, 'Let there be . . .' and it was so."

The Word Is Christ

Supremely, the Word is Christ—Christ who has a part in creation, Christ who is preached by men, Christ who is the center of the Bible.

"When a man has a thought, a word, or a conversation within himself, he speaks to himself incessantly and is full of words that suggest counsel as to what to do or not to do. He continually converses and deliberates on this within himself. And particularly when something is close to his heart and makes him angry or happy, his heart is so full of anger and so full of happiness that his emotions involuntarily spill over into his mouth. For a word is not merely the utterance of the mouth; rather is is the thought of the heart. . . .

"Thus God too from all eternity has a Word, a speech, a thought, or a conversation with Himself in His divine heart, unknown to angels and men. This is called His Word. From eternity He was within God's paternal heart, and through Him God resolved to create heaven and earth. But no man was aware of such a resolve until the Word became flesh and proclaimed this to us."[51]

This Word is essentially the Word of promise, the promise of the forgiveness of sins in Jesus Christ. It is the living statement that God is willing to justify sinful men, not because they deserve it but because He is the loving and merciful God who cares for men and wishes for their fellowship. All this God does in spite

36

of man's sin. The Word is the objective ground of justification: faith is the subjective response to that Word.

"For God does not deal, nor has He ever dealt, with man otherwise than through the Word of promise. . . . We in turn cannot deal with God otherwise than through faith in the Word of His promise." [52]

"To this promise belongs faith; namely, that I believe that I shall receive what is promised to me, and a pledge of the promise whereby promise and faith are joined together. Where there is no promise, there is no faith; and where there is no faith, the promise is nothing. And since God clearly makes this promise to us gratis, without any merit or work on our part (for otherwise it would not be a promise but a reward or recompense), the promise is therefore received and accepted only by faith, without any works; otherwise our works would merit the promise. Therefore one satisfies the promise by faith, and faith is satisfied by the promise." [53]

The Work of the Word

Faith is created in a man by his hearing the Word, the Word of God, the Word of justification, the promise of the forgiveness of sins in Jesus Christ, the Word which comes to him through the Bible, through faithful preaching, the Word which works within him.

God's "Word should be allowed to work alone, without our work and interference. Why? Because it is not in my power to fashion the hearts of men as the potter molds the clay and fashion them at my pleasure. I can get no further than their ears; their hearts I cannot reach. And since I cannot pour faith into their hearts, I cannot, nor should I, force any one to have faith. That is God's work alone, who causes faith to live in the heart. . . . We should preach the Word, but the results must be left solely to God's good pleasure." [54]

Faith Takes God at His Word

To have faith means to take God at His Word. Whatever God says is true and can be trusted absolutely. It is for this reason that

Luther gave the following advice: "Provide yourself with armor from Scripture concerning justification, which takes place through faith. Collect, I say, a number of Scripture passages that ascribe righteousness to God. Then, if you put your reliance on these passages, you will be able to stand even after a fall." [55]

Why? Because they speak of God's forgiveness in Jesus Christ. Faith means to take God at His Word, even if it means going against all known experience. Faith is complete surrender to God.

"The art of faith consists in this that we apprehend what we do not see. In fact, all that we have from Christ is hidden from view; what we see is opposite. Faith sees the intangible, that which is not felt or apprehended. That is the skill of faith. It has sharp vision, enabling me to perceive life when death stares me in the face. . . . All this I see and feel, and yet faith also sees life and says: 'Even though I am being killed, I shall live again.' " [56]

Faith is audacious confidence in God, the implicit trust that He will do as He has said. "This is the nature of faith that it boldly takes the grace of God for granted, forms an opinion of confidence toward Him, and feels assured that God will regard him favorably and not to forsake him. . . . Faith does not require information, knowledge, certainty, but free submission and joyful venturing upon God's unfelt, untried, and unrecognized goodness." [57]

IV

Faith cannot be understood as anything other than faith in Christ.[58]

Theses 26-29: "For these two propositions battle against each other: Christ was delivered to make satisfaction for our sins; and we ourselves are justified from our sins through the law [i. e., works of the law]. For either He was not delivered for our sins, or we are not justified from our sins through the law.

"The Scriptures, however, proclaim that the transgressions of us all have been laid on Him, and He was smitten for the sins of God's people, and by His bruise we are healed (Isaiah 53:4-6; 1 Peter 2:24). But having been justified by grace in this way, we do then do works, yes, Christ Himself does all in us." [59]

Faith Rests on Christ

Luther never tires of explaining that our faith is in Christ and in Christ alone. Faith "produces a daring and courage which enables one to hold anything on earth in contempt, to fear nothing at all, but in gay defiance depend only on Christ." [60]

"Our faith is to rest on Christ, and on nothing else." [61] "In my heart there reigns, and shall ever reign, this one article, namely, that faith in my dear Lord Christ, which is the sole beginning, middle, and end of all spiritual and godly thoughts which I might have at any one time, day or night." [62]

"One must close one's eyes to all teachings, and the only thought and way of justification to which one must cling is this, that it takes place through Christ." [63]

"For faith does not err or stray; but wherever the Christ is to whom it adheres, there it also must be and remain. And the stronger the faith is, the more surely this Way is traveled. For this walking is nothing but a constant growth in faith and in an ever stronger assurance of eternal life in Christ." [64]

There is no cause for concern over the possibility of a weak faith or a strong faith, because faith in itself is unimportant: its importance is in its object—Jesus Christ.

When Faith Is Feeble

"All that is Christ's is mine. Through Him we acquire all His goods and eternal life. Even if my faith is feeble, I still have the self-same treasure and the self-same Christ that others have. There is no difference. . . .

"We might compare this to two persons who possess a hundred guldens. The one may carry them in a paper sack, the other may keep them in an iron chest. But for all that, both possess the entire treasure. Thus the Christ whom you and I own is one and the same, regardless of the strength or weakness of your faith or of mine." [65]

Faith is in Christ and in Christ alone; to say anything to the contrary is to utter blasphemy.

Theses 69-71: "But who can bear this blasphemy that our works beget us, or that we are the creatures of our works? In that case it would be permissible to say, contrary to the prophet, 'We have made ourselves, and God has not created us' (Malachi 2:10; Psalm 100:3). It is accordingly as blasphemous to say that a man is his own god, creator, or producer as it is blasphemous to say that he is justified by his own works." [66]

Justification is not something that we do for ourselves, with or without God's help. It is throughout something which God alone does in us and for us.

Two Alternatives

And here we have come full circle in Luther's thought concerning faith. There are simply two alternatives which face man — faith or unfaith, worship or blasphemy.

"Whoever is an orator, let him develop this topic. He will see that faith is something omnipotent and that its power is inestimable and infinite, for it attributes glory to God, which is the highest thing that can be attributed to Him.

"To attribute glory to God is to believe in Him, to regard Him as truthful, wise, righteous, merciful, and almighty; in short, to acknowledge Him as the Author and Donor of every good. . . . Therefore faith justifies, because it renders to God what is due to Him." [67]

Faith is to give all honor and glory to God by believing in His Son, whom He has sent for our sins. Faith is in Christ: faith *is* Christ.

"Christian faith is not an idle quality or an empty husk in the heart . . . it is a sure trust and firm acceptance in the heart. It takes hold of Christ in such a way that Christ is the object of faith, or rather not the object but, so to speak, the One who is present in the faith itself. Thus faith is a sort of knowledge or darkness that nothing can see.

"Yet the Christ of whom faith takes hold is sitting in this darkness as God sat in the darkness on Sinai and in the temple. Therefore our 'formal righteousness' [68] is not a love that informs faith, but it is faith itself, a cloud in our hearts; that is, trust in a thing we do not see, in Christ, who is present especially when He cannot be seen." [69]

Not a Subjective Emotional Experience

Luther's formula "justification by faith alone" is often misunderstood and misinterpreted for the reason that no real investigation is made into what Luther meant by it. From the verbal formula it would be possible to claim that it represents a subjective emotional experience, but, as we have seen, that is not what Luther meant.

Admittedly the formula itself does not include any specific reference to Christ, and it is often criticized on this ground, perhaps rightly so, but for Luther, faith and justification have no meaning except in Christ.

We began by quoting Karl Barth, and so we conclude: "This is the motivation of faith; something is 'moved,' and something really 'takes' place. By God's Word, together with the life-giving power and the unique sovereignty of the Spirit, one man among many is permitted to exist continually as a free man. . . . He is freed to put his whole joyful trust in this Word and to become unreservedly obedient to what this announcement of God Himself expresses about His love for the world, His people, and also for the theologian.

"No one can take such action by his own power. A man can do this only when he is overcome by God's Word and its Spirit of power, when he is resurrected and recreated by it for such an act." [70]

Chapter Four

Ex Operatum

A Lutheran professor of systematic theology recently referred to the relationship between faith and works as being "one of the knottiest problems in Lutheran theology." [1] Behind this statement lies the fact of the bitter controversy which shook the Lutheran Church to its roots soon after Luther's death. [2]

Following the lead given by Philip Melanchthon, several Wittenberg theologians began to insist that justification without good works was an impossibility. Immediately there was a reaction from other Wittenberg theologians who insisted, with equal determination, that justification was by faith, and by faith alone. And, as so often happens, each side in its zeal to confound the opposition found itself in intractable extremes.

Opposing Views

On the one hand, there was George Major insisting: "I do confess that I have hitherto taught, and still teach, and henceforth will teach all my life that good works are necessary to salvation. And I declare publicly and with clear and plain words that no one is saved by evil works and also that no one is saved without good works." [3]

And on the other hand, Nicolas von Amsdorf was insisting, "This proposition: Good works are injurious to salvation, is a correct, true, Christian proposition, taught and preached by St. Paul and Luther." [4]

But neither Major nor Amsdorf had understood what Luther had meant when he spoke of faith and works.

The seeds of this particular controversy were sown during

Luther's lifetime. He was continually being misinterpreted, misrepresented, and attacked for his strong views concerning works — good or otherwise.

The Protestant humanist Wilibald Pirkheimer complained in 1528: "Like Dürer, I was at first a good Lutheran. We hoped things would be better than in the Roman Church, but the Lutherans are worse. The former were hypocrites; the latter openly live disgraceful lives. For Justification by Faith alone is not possible. Without works faith is dead. Luther, with his bold, petulant tongue, has either fallen under a delusion or else is being led astray by the Evil One." [5]

About 3 years earlier the Catholic humanist Erasmus had commented in a letter: "The two parties are dragging at the opposite ends of a rope. When it breaks, they will both fall onto their backs. . . . Laymen need not puzzle themselves with conundrums. Whether works justify or faith justifies matters little since all allow that faith will not save without good works." [6]

But again, neither man had understood Luther.

Luther's View of Good Works

The main line of criticism against Luther was, and often still is, that he was of the opinion that good works should be suppressed. But nothing could be further from Luther's intention.

In his great treatise *On Good Works* of 1520 he complains: "When I exalt faith and reject such works done without faith, they accuse me of forbidding good works. The fact of the matter is that I want very much to teach the real good works which spring from faith." [7]

But the problem was the one with which we are now familiar: old vocabulary filled with new content. For what Luther meant by good works was a far cry from what traditional Catholicism meant by the term.

On June 15, 1520, Pope Leo X issued the papal bull *Exurge Domine* [8] against the teaching of Luther. In it were condemned 41 statements taken from Luther's writings, and these were described as "poisonous," "pernicious," "scandalous," "seductive to godly and simple minds, and . . . contrary to all love and reverence for the holy Roman Church." [9]

One statement that gave particular offense was number 31: "In every good work the righteous man sins." [10] This was a sentence taken from Luther's *Explanation of the Articles Debated at Leipzig.* (1519) [11]

The View of the Roman Church

This statement was particularly offensive because traditionally the holy Roman Church regarded justification as the renewal of man, the gradual metamorphosis of the sinner into the very image of God. The mechanics of this transformation were seen to be action by God supplemented by action by man. Through power given by God man is assisted to fulfill all the demands of the Law in love and obedience.

Thus Catholic piety is expressed in a continuous striving to perfect this life by an all-out effort to conform to the law of God. Therefore a man is righteous because of his works of humility, love, and obedience.

But Luther objects, and this is the storm center of the Reformation: A Christian's confidence before God does not depend on anything he has done or is doing because his highest attainments are imperfect. A Christian's confidence is in what God has done in Christ for him.

Luther responded negatively to the papal bull, which had ordered the burning of his books, by making a bonfire of papal books, canon law, and the bull itself. His more positive response came in the form of four works defending the articles condemned in the bull. The last and most important of these works was the *Defense and Explanation of all the Articles of Dr. Martin Luther Which Were Unjustly Condemned by the Roman Bull.* (1521) [12]

Good Works Not Adequate

Here Luther defends the 31st article, that "in every good work the righteous man sins," as follows: "This article annoys the great saints of work righteousness, who place their trust not in God's mercy but in their own righteousness, that is, on sand. . . ."[13] But a godly Christian ought to learn and know that

44

all his good works are inadequate and insufficient in the sight of God. In the company of all the dear saints he ought to despair of his own works and rely solely on the mercy of God, putting all confidence and trust in Him.

"Therefore we want to establish this article very firmly and see what the dear saints have to say about it. Isaiah 64[:6] says, 'We are all of us unclean, and all our righteousness is as a filthy stinking rag.' You notice that the prophet makes no exceptions . . . if our righteousness is unclean and stinking before God, what will our unrighteousness be? . . . Now if there is such a thing as a good work without sin, this prophet lies, which God forbid! Is not this passage from Isaiah sufficiently clear? Why then do they condemn my article, which says nothing but what Isaiah says?"

He then goes on to quote in a similar vein Ecclesiastes 7:20, Psalm 143:2, Augustine's *Confessions,* Book IX, and Gregory the Great's *Moralia,* IX (which in turn quotes Job 9:3 and 15). Luther concludes: "If these passages do not help to substantiate my article, then may God help it! I would much rather be condemned with Isaiah, David, Solomon, Paul, Augustine, and Gregory than praised with the pope and all the bishops and papists, even though all the world were made up of pope, bishops, and papists." [14]

In Luther's eyes traditional Catholicism was guilty of putting the cart before the horse when it insisted that works make a Christian's life valid before God. In opposition he insisted that it is the Christian who makes the works good, not that good works make the Christian.

And this is not simply a theological conondrum of no significance to the layman, as Erasmus believed. It is of profound significance, because it represents the difference between living under the constraint of the Law and living within the freedom of the Spirit.

Good Works Not Pure

The core of Luther's reasoning against the papal bull is found in this passage: "Back in the first two articles [15] I have shown

45

that all the saints struggle against their sinful flesh and continue to be sinners as long as they live in the flesh, which is at war with the Spirit. At one and the same time they serve God according to the spirit, and sin according to the flesh. If, then, a godly man is at the same time justified by reason of the spirit, and sinful by reason of the flesh, his work must be like the person, the fruit like the trees. Insofar as the spirit participates in the work, it is good; insofar as the flesh participates in it, it is evil, for Christ says, 'A good tree bears good fruit; an evil tree bears evil fruit' [Matthew 7:17]. God always judges the work according to the person, as it is written in Genesis 4 [:4], 'And the Lord had regard for Abel and his offering, but for Cain and his offering He had no regard.' First He looks at Abel and Cain, only afterward at their offerings. And here too, since the person is not altogether pure, the work can never be altogether pure. If the author is not altogether competent, the work will not be entirely competent either. Every work must be like its author; this is the common consent of reason and experience." [16]

Trust in Good Works Is Sinful

Here we are back with Luther's understanding of the radical nature of sin. The nature of man is not like the proverbial curate's egg, good in parts, as traditional Catholicism held. The natural condition of man, as we saw in the previous chapter, is that he is in helpless separation from God, that is, in unbelief, and whatever he does—good or ill—he is helplessly on the wrong side of God. To think that doing the right things will win God's favor only makes the matter worse.

"The person who believes that he can obtain grace by doing what is in him adds sin to sin, so that he becomes doubly guilty." [17] What Luther means by this is that this attitude is a refusal to face up to the fact of our sinful nature, and, instead of liberating man from himself, it serves to harden him in his opposition to God.

"To trust in works . . . is equivalent to giving one's self the honor and taking it from God, to whom fear is due in connection with every work. But this is wrong, namely, to please one's self,

46

to enjoy one's self in one's own works, and to adore one's self as an idol. He who is self-confident and without fear of God acts entirely in this matter. For if he had fear, he would not be self-confident, and for this reason he would not be pleased with himself; he would be pleased with God." [18]

We Sin Because We Are Sinners

The church of Luther's day taught that man was essentially good, like the stem of a tree; his sins were like unwanted growths which needed to be pruned away so that the budding good works might flower. But in contrast Luther maintained that when the root is rotten, no amount of pruning will ever improve the tree.

Commenting on Psalm 51, he explains David's meaning as being: "'I am a sinner, not because I have committed adultery nor because I have had Uriah murdered. But I have committed adultery and murder because I was born, indeed conceived and formed in the womb, as a sinner.' So we are not sinners because we commit this or that sin, but we commit them because we are sinners first. That is, a bad tree and a bad seed also bring forth bad fruits, and from a bad root only a bad tree can grow." [19]

For Luther, therefore, it is the height of spiritual arrogance and religious anarchy to insist that we can by some effort on our part become what God wants us to be and, therefore, acceptable to Him.[20]

"A god of this kind . . . cannot be found anywhere. Therefore it is all a vain imagination and dream, the invention of an idol in the heart. For nowhere has God promised that He intends to justify men on account of religious orders, observances, and forms of worship that have been thought up by men.

"In fact, as all Scripture attests, nothing is more abominable to God than such self-chosen works and forms of worship. . . . Therefore all who trust in their own ability and righteousness are serving a god who by nature is no god but is a god only in their opinion." [21]

Popular Belief

Popular Catholicism had continually taught that regular

attendance at Mass and confession, giving alms, abstaining from meat on Fridays, telling one's beads, and so on were the kind of thing that God noticed in a person's life. Best of all was to become a monk or nun, so that the whole of life could be devoted to the performance of these good works. All this Luther knew from bitter experience in the Augustinian priory.

And even the purged Catholicism of Erasmus was no different in this matter. In the year 1524 he published what was virtually a treatise on justification. It was called *Concerning the Immense Mercy of God*.[22] The following quotations are taken from this work to illustrate Erasmus' thinking with regard to good works:

"It is wiser to win immortality with a little suffering. All who persist in sin are foolish; those who amend their lives are wise."[23] "If a king forgave a group of traitors and only warned them to mend their ways in the future, he would be claimed merciful, since he did not punish or fine them. God actually offers a reward for mending our ways."[24]

"David had so many other excellent virtues that, considering these, his sin could be forgiven. He gave up the luxuries of his court. He wore sackcloth, and he ate ashes and wept so much every night that his bedding was soaked."[25] "I shall . . . show you how God's mercy can best be obtained . . . prayers, tears, fasting, sackcloth, and ashes. These things do indeed obtain His mercy for us, but kindness to our neighbor actually—if I may use the expression—wrests it from Him."[26]

"Whatever kindness we show our neighbor the Lord takes note of. . . . He promises to repay them with interest. If you wish to become rich in heavenly goods, you should do business with this great Lender."[27] "God is appeased by several forms of sacrifice, spiritual hymns, songs, prayers, watchings, fastings, poor clothing; but no sacrifice is more effective than mercy toward your brother."[28]

"Give alms to a poor man, and it will deliver you from all evil, for a treasure cannot be buried more safely than in the heart of a poor man. . . . Your alms-giving will not remain silent in your hour of need but will cry out in your behalf."[29]

The Knowledge of Christ

But if this is Christianity, Luther will want to know where Christ comes in it all and whether there is any difference between Christianity and other religions. "The Turk thinks the very same as the Carthusian, namely, 'If I do this or that, I have a God who is favorably disposed toward me; if I do not, I have a God who is wrathful.' There is no middle ground between human working and the knowledge of Christ; if this knowledge is obscured, it does not matter whether you become a monk or a heathen afterward." [30]

To assert that man's actions influence God's attitude is to underestimate the totality of sin,[31] to overestimate man's capacity to act freely,[32] and to shift the emphasis from God to man in the matter of salvation.[33] Luther finds this astounding, and he comments ironically that if anyone is physically ill, the first thing he does is to rush to God and implore Him to restore him to full health. Yet in his desperate spiritual illness he runs away from God and refuses to return to Him until he has healed himself.

Luther concludes: "If you want to be cured of sin, you must not withdraw from God but run to Him and pray to Him with much more confidence than if some physical distress had overtaken you. God is not hostile to sinners, only to unbelievers. That means to those who do not recognize and bewail their sin or seek help for it from God but in their own presumption wish first to purify themselves, will not admit their need of His grace, and will not suffer Him to be a God who gives to everyone and takes nothing for what He gives." [34]

In his famous treatise *The Freedom of a Christian* (1520) Dr. Martin makes the following statement concerning works: "If works are sought after as a means to righteousness, are burdened with this perverse leviathan, and are done under the false impression that through them one is justified, they are made necessary, and freedom and faith are destroyed; and this addition to them makes them no longer good but truly damnable works.

"They are not free, and they blaspheme the grace of God, since to justify and to save by faith belongs to the grace of God

alone. What the works have no power to do, they themselves—
by a godless presumption through this folly of ours—pretend to
do and thus violently force themselves into the office and glory
of grace.

How Faith and Works Relate

"We do not, therefore, reject good works; on the contrary,
we cherish and teach them as much as possible. We do not condemn them for their own sake but on account of this godless
addition to them and the perverse idea that righteousness is to
be sought through them, for that makes them appear good out-
wardly, when in truth they are not good. They deceive men and
lead them to deceive one another like ravening wolves in sheep's
clothing [Matthew 7:15]." [35]

And here we have come to the distinctive feature of Luther's
thinking concerning works. In justification, works are completely
neutral: [36] works are but the external indication of the internal
state of the heart of man; [37] that is, a man is not necessarily better
with them or worse without them.[38] Works are bad only if they
are relied on to win favor with God; [39] works are good only if
they spring from faith.[40]

"In this faith all works become equal, and one work is like
another; all distinctions between works fall away, whether they
be great, small, short, long, many, or few. For the works are not
acceptable for their own sake but because of faith, which is
always the same and lives and works in each and every work
without distinction, however numerous and varied these works
always are, just as all the members of the body live, work, and
take their name from the head, and without the head no member
can live, work, or have a name." [41]

Therefore, to confuse the issue between faith and works is to
commit spiritual suicide, and this is just what Luther wants to
prevent at all costs. "I constantly dwell on the doctrine of justification that you may thoroughly understand it and differentiate
between faith and good works. . . . Faith gives one eternal life, for
it gives one Him who is eternal Life and the Bread of Life." [42]

"This faith cannot exist in connection with works—that is

to say, if you at the same time claim to be justified by works, whatever their character—for that would be the same as 'limping with two different opinions' [I Kings 18:21], as worshiping Baal and kissing one's own hand [Job 31:27-28], which, as Job says, is a very great iniquity. Therefore the moment you begin to have faith you learn that all things in you are altogether blameworthy, sinful, and damnable, as the apostle says in Romans 3 [:23], 'Since all have sinned and fall short of the glory of God,' and 'None is righteous, no, not one . . . all have turned aside, together they have gone wrong' [Romans 3:10-12].

"When you have learned this, you will know that you need Christ, who suffered and rose again for you, so that, if you believe in Him, you may through this faith become a new man insofar as your sins are forgiven and you are justified by the merits of another, namely, Christ alone." [43]

The Heart of the Matter

It is not what works are before God but what a man is before God that is at the heart of the matter.[44] A man's standing before God does not depend on anything that he has been able to do but rests entirely on what God in Christ has already done on his behalf, and his response is simply one of faith, one of acceptance.

"Since, then, works justify no one and a man must be righteous before a good work, it is very evident that it is faith alone which, because of the pure mercy of God through Christ and in His Word, worthily and sufficiently justifies and saves the person." [45]

"This is the righteousness of Christ and the Holy Spirit, which we do not perform but receive, which we do not have but accept, when God the Father grants it to us through Jesus Christ." [46]

It is by faith and by faith alone that a man is justified, but in his treatise *On Good Works* Luther slightly clouds the issue by speaking of faith as "the chief work." [47] But it soon becomes clear that he is speaking against the background of John 6:29, where Jesus answers the Jews, who wanted to know what they should be doing to do the work of God, with the reply: "This is the work of God, that you believe in Him whom He has sent."

Luther maintains that "a man can find God by no other work than faith and trust; a man can lose God by no other work than unbelief." [48] From beginning to end faith can only be in and from Christ alone. "But if you ask where faith and confidence may be found or whence they come, it is certainly the most necessary thing to know. First, without any doubt it does not come from your works or from your merits, but only from Jesus Christ, freely promised and freely given. . . .

"Faith, therefore, does not originate in works; neither do works create faith, but faith must spring up and flow from the blood and wounds and death of Christ. . . . We never read that the Holy Spirit was given to anybody because he had performed some works but always when men have heard the Gospel of Christ and the mercy of God. Faith must arise at all times from this same Word and from no other source—and in our own day too." [49]

With this in mind Luther can speak of faith as the "master-workman and captain" of all other works, [50] or as "the fore-man," [51] because faith is the source of all good works, and if there is no faith, there are no works. "It is clear, then, that a Christian has all he needs in faith and needs no works to justify him." [52]

Good Works Follow Faith

But having stated this, Luther never meant to say that works are insignificant or unnecessary. Luther "never intended to say that true faith is, or ever could be—much less should be—without good works. His point was not that faith is never 'alone' but that 'only' faith without works—hence the term 'faith alone'—is necessary for justification before God." [53]

And even though the Reformer had a low opinion of the Epistle of James—an opinion which has drawn a flood of critical ink—he nonetheless accepted its main teaching: "Faith without works is dead." [54] "If good works do not follow, it is certain that this faith in Christ does not dwell in your heart but that dead faith. . . . All who boast of works to justify themselves in the eyes of God show that they understand nothing about Christ or faith." [55]

The good works that Luther talks about incessantly are not the works that are imposed by the church. The monastic habit, dietary laws, scrupulous attendance at Mass and confession — all these sort of things are not good works as far as Luther is concerned. The good works he talks about are the spontaneous actions of love and honesty, untarnished by selfish ambition, which flow naturally from the Christian as he goes about his daily affairs.

"A Christian man who lives in this confidence [of faith] toward God knows all things, can do all things, ventures everything that needs to be done, and does everything gladly and willingly, not that he may gather merits and good works, but because it is a pleasure for him to please God in doing these things. He simply serves God with no thought of reward, content that his service pleases God." [56]

The recurring theme of Luther's thinking concerning works is based on Matthew 7:17-20: "So every sound tree bears good fruit, but the bad tree bears evil fruit. A sound tree cannot bear evil fruit, nor can a bad tree bear good fruit. . . . Thus you will know them by their fruits." [57] The following two quotations will show something of the varied ways he expresses this insight.

"We should think of the works of a Christian who is justified and saved by faith because of the pure and free mercy of God, just as we should think of the works which Adam and Eve did in Paradise and all their children would have done if they had not sinned. . . . Now Adam was created righteous and upright without sin by God so that he had no need of being justified and made upright through his tilling and keeping the garden; but, that he might not be idle, the Lord gave him a task to do, to cultivate and protect the garden. This task would truly have been the freest of works, done only to please God and not to obtain righteousness, which Adam already had in full measure. . . .

"A bishop, when he consecrates a church, confirms children, or performs some other duty belonging to his office, is not made a bishop by these works. Indeed, if he had not first been made a bishop, none of these works would be valid. . . . So the Christian who is consecrated by his faith does good works, but the works do not make him holier or more Christian, for that is the work of faith alone." [58]

The Case of Nicodemus

Luther comments on John 3:3 that it is "as if He [Christ] were to say: 'Do not imagine, Nicodemus, that you are saved by reason of your honesty and piety. Admittedly, one must live honestly, decently, and usefully in this world. If you do not, then Master Jack, the executioner, will appear on the scene with his sword and rope. He will say: 'What you do not want to do you will be compelled to do!'

"But if you suppose that your good works are going to attain the kingdom of heaven for you, you will find them of no value. For these works and this piety give nothing but this temporal life to you. Thanks to them, you are not throttled or banished from house and home, wife and child, or hanged on the gallows. Thus if you are a citizen of Jerusalem, you can enjoy life, honor, and fame by reason of your respectability.

"But so far as the kingdom of heaven, the church, and the kingdom of Christ are concerned you must remember to become a new man. You must think of yourself as an infant which as yet is not only incapable of a single work but, in fact, does not yet have life and existence.

"Therefore Christ says to Nicodemus: 'I have come to proclaim a different doctrine, namely, how you must be reborn to become good. To be sure, Holy Writ has contained and defined this proclamation all along, but you do not read it. Even if you do, you fail to understand the message that you must be born anew before you can perform good works. For sinners beget none but sinners; the person is corrupt.'

Faith Is Busy and Active

"In Matthew 7:17 and 16 the Lord declares: 'A bad tree can bear no good fruit; thistles do not bear figs, nor thorns grapes.' " [59]

Even though works have their source in faith, they should not

54

be trusted for their own sake,[60] because they result not from our own natural abilities but from the graciousness of God. Both our inner faith and its outer manifestation in works are God's work within us.

In his famous "Preface to the Epistle to the Romans" our Reformer writes: "Faith . . . is a divine work in us which changes us and makes us to be born anew of God, John 1 [:12-13]. It kills the old Adam and makes us altogether different men, in heart and spirit and mind and powers; and it brings with it the Holy Spirit.

"Oh, it is a living, busy, active, mighty thing, this faith. It is impossible for it not to be doing good works incessantly. It does not ask whether good works are to be done, but before the question has been asked, it has already done them and is constantly doing them. . . . Faith is a living, daring confidence in God's grace, so sure and so certain that the believer would stake his life on it a thousand times.

"This knowledge of and confidence in God's grace makes men glad and bold and happy in dealing with God and with all creatures. And this is the work which the Holy Spirit performs in faith. Because of it, without compulsion, a person is ready and glad to do good to everyone, to suffer everything, out of love and praise to God, who has shown him this grace.

"Thus it is impossible to separate works from faith, quite as impossible as to separate heat and light from fire. . . . Pray God that He may work faith in you. Otherwise you will surely remain forever without faith, regardless of what you may think or do." [61]

The relationship between faith and works may seem to some to be "one of the knottiest problems of Lutheran theology," or to others merely "a theological conundrum," but to Luther it is basic and vital. For him the justification of the sinner is a work accomplished by God Himself through His Son Jesus Christ pouring out His life unto death.

Efficacy of Christ's Cross Denied
by Work Righteousness

Therefore to say that the works of man can satisfy God is to deny the efficacy of Christ's cross and God's initiative in salvation. "He who presumes that he is righteous in any other way than by believing in Christ rejects Christ and considers Christ's passion and resurrection useless." [62]

If a man can do the necessary things that will secure his justification from God, then Christ died in vain. "A fine honoring of Christ's death, to say that it is helped by our works, and whatever it does our works can do — so that we are His equal in strength and goodness! This is the very devil; he can never quit abusing the blood of Christ. The matter itself in its very core, then, demands that we say, 'Faith alone justifies.' " [63]

"Faith is, as it were, the center of a circle. If anybody strays from the center, it is impossible for him to have the circle round him, and he must blunder. The center is Christ." [64]

Chapter Five

Per Christum

Luther wrote all kinds of things — sermons, tracts, hymns, treatises — but in all this tremendous output there is one category that is absent. Unlike Calvin, Luther did not make a systematic presentation of his theology. The need was certainly felt, for after his death the first edition of the *Tischreden (Table Talk)* was issued as a compendium of Luther's theology in topical form.[1]

It could be argued that his temperament was not entirely suited for producing such a work, and, anyway, the sheer pressure of his Reformation activities did not allow him the leisure to do so; many of his projected writings were never completed.[2]

However, Luther's closest colleague, Philip Melanchthon, did write such a theological textbook, published in 1521 under the title *Loci communes rerum theologicorum (Basic Theological Doctrines)*. Luther greeted it as a masterpiece of evangelical theology, declaring it a "little book which in my judgment deserves not only to be immortalized but even canonized."[3] Later he expressed the opinion: "There's no book under the sun in which the whole of theology is so compactly presented as in the *Loci Communes.* . . . No better book has been written after the Holy Scriptures than Philip's. He expresses himself more concisely than I do when he argues and instructs. I'm garrulous and more rhetorical."[4]

Melanchthon's opening sentence of his treatment of justification in his *Loci* is a compact and concise statement of Luther's teaching on the doctrine: "We are justified when, put to death by the law, we are made alive again by the word of grace promised in *Christ;* the Gospel forgives our sins, and we cling to *Christ* in faith, not doubting in the least that the righteousness of *Christ* is our righteousness, that the satisfaction *Christ* wrought for our expiation and that the resurrection of *Christ* is ours." [5]

What is significant about this statement is that Melanchthon, for all his precision and lack of Luther's rhetorical fullness, cannot speak about justification without stressing, at five particular points, that the doctrine is meaningless without Christ. Yet it is in this particular area that Luther has been persistently misunderstood and misrepresented.

Justification Is in Christ

Luther never taught that justification is merely a bald transaction by God within the individual. Nor did he teach that when an individual simply comes to believe that he is justified his salvation is sure, without any reference to the personal presence of the indwelling Christ, or to His satisfaction of the cross. The formulas *sola fide* and *justification by faith alone* may give this impression, but it must be remembered that these were shorthand summaries of the doctrine, and although the omission of the words "in Christ" may have been misleading, they were always implied.

Luther was only too aware of the problem. He wrote: "Among the distinguished teachers there are some who say that forgiveness of sins and justification by grace consist entirely on divine imputation, that is, in God's accounting it sufficient that he to whom He reckons or does not reckon sin is justified or not justified from his sins by this. . . . If this were true, the whole New Testament would be nothing and in vain. And Christ would have labored foolishly and uselessly by suffering for sin. Then even God Himself would have practiced mere humbug and trickery unnecessarily. . . . Against this horrible, terrible understanding and error the holy apostle has the custom of always referring to faith *in Christ.*" [6]

This was vitally important to Luther because there was a time in his life when he did not understand the person of Christ: he once regarded Him as another Moses, who made impossible demands on mankind. Speaking of his early days in the monastery, he reflects, "I did not [then] believe in Christ; I regarded Him only as a severe and terrible Judge, portrayed as seated on a rainbow. . . . I did not know Christ and did not seek in and through Him what I wanted." [7]

The so-called "tower-experience," whenever it occurred, was not simply a discovery of the doctrine of justification but also the simultaneous encounter with Christ the Redeemer, who stands at the center of the Scriptures. Thus Luther came to understand that to believe in Christ without a true understanding of justification is to believe in a false Christ, and that a doctrine of justification that is not centered in Christ is a false doctrine.[8]

The Uniqueness of Christ

In his exposition of the First Commandment in his Large Catechism Luther explained, "As I have often said, the trust and faith of the heart alone make both God and an idol. If your faith and trust are right, then your God is the true God. On the other hand, if your trust is false and wrong, then you have not the true God." [9]

If we are to ask the question: How can we be certain that we believe in the true God, Dr. Martin will answer: "This is the article of justification. The Holy Spirit insists that we never teach, know of, think of, hear, or accept any other god than this God, whose flesh and blood we imprint and hold in our hearts if we want to be saved. . . . If you want to be saved, then admit no God other than the Son of Man." [10]

This uniqueness of Christ is at the heart of Luther's theology, although it is debatable whether one should speak of Luther's *theology* or of Luther's *Christology,* because for him the knowledge of God comes only through a knowledge of Jesus Christ.

Christ is the only security for the believer that he is accepted by God; [11] Christ is the only object of faith; [12] and Christ is the only "ship or passage," [13] the only way to God the Father.

Commenting on a number of passages, including John 14:6, he writes: "These and similar pronouncements of Scripture are clearer than the light of day and are utterly reliable. The Scrip-

59

tures clearly compel us to condemn whatever is only a matter of rules, statutes, orders, schools of thought, and, in addition, whatever falls short of, is contrary to, or goes beyond Christ, even if these things had been handed over by angels from heaven or confirmed by mighty miracles. He who said, 'I am the Way,' will not allow another way to be chosen. By these words He has rescinded all other ways, past, present, and future. He has made them null and void. He who said, 'Hear Him,' does not permit another leader or master to arise, whether he tries to offer anything better or worse. Any law or tradition apart from Christ is condemned by these words." [14]

On the basis of John 1:51 Luther frequently compared the person and work of Christ to Jacob's ladder in Genesis 28. "For why should the man Christ have been given us as a ladder to the Father if we ignore Him and bypass Him and presume to ascend to heaven and measure God's judgment by our own reason?" [15]

"For Christ must be all — the beginning, the middle, and the end of our salvation. He must be the first stone, the stone on which other stones are placed and on which the entire vault or roof is constructed [see 1 Peter 2:4-10]. He is the first, middle, and last rung of the ladder to heaven. For through Him we must make the beginning, continue, and conclude our journey into yonder life." [16]

Another's Righteousness

The basis for Luther's confidence in Christ is this: mankind is helplessly lost in sin, unable to reach the standard of righteousness demanded by God's law, but in the fullness of time God's own sinless Son came into the world and fulfilled all the demands of righteousness on behalf of mankind.

Hence, "when we come to the doctrine of righteousness in the sight of God, we should simply reject all Law as useless for our justification and admit nothing but the law of the Spirit, the promise that Jesus died on account of our sins. This is the Word of grace and promise, which does not demand anything of us as in the Law but offers plenary satisfaction through the perfect victim, Christ, the victim who put an end to Moses and the whole Law." [17]

The righteousness of Christ is His one, complete, perfect sacrifice and satisfaction on the cross where He died in the place of sinners. Sinners have no rights before the holy God except the right of judgment and condemnation.

Therefore, says Luther, "we cannot deal with God on our own initiative, for we are children of wrath (Ephesians 2:3). We must have someone else through whom we can come before God—someone to represent us and to reconcile us with God. And there is no other Mediator than the Lord Christ, who is the Son of God. . . . We must bring Christ [to God], come with Him, pay God with Him, and carry out all our dealings through Him and with Him." [18] "Sprinkle me, therefore, with the true goat's blood of Jesus Christ. Then I will be truly and thoroughly cleansed without all my works and efforts." [19]

The Great Exchange

Forgiveness of sins, justification, and the application of righteousness become effective in what has been termed "the Great Exchange." The sinner's sin rests on Christ, and His righteousness rests on the justified sinner.

"Learn Christ and Him crucified. Learn to praise Him, and, despairing of yourself, say, 'Lord Jesus, You are my righteousness, just as I am Your sin. You have taken upon Yourself what You were not and have given to me what I was not.' " [20] Therefore the life of the Christian is hidden in the righteousness of Christ.

"It follows now that the man who is righteous through faith does not through himself give to anyone what is his; he does this through Another, namely, Jesus Christ, who alone is so righteous as to render to all what should be rendered to them. As a matter of fact, they owe everything to Him. But he who believes in Christ and by the spirit of faith has become one with Him not only renders satisfaction now to all but also brings it about that they owe everything to him, since he has all things in common with Christ. His sins are no longer his; they are Christ's. But in Christ sins are unable to overcome righteousness. In fact, they themselves are overcome. Hence they are destroyed in Him.

Again, Christ's righteousness now belongs not only to Christ; it belongs to His Christian. Therefore the Christian cannot owe anything to anyone or be oppressed by his sins, since he is supported by such great righteousness." [21]

This righteousness of Christ becomes real in the life of the Christian by faith, for this "righteousness is identical with faith and comes through faith." [22] And thus Luther is able to say with confidence: "I am Christ, that is to say, Christ's righteousness, victory, life, etc., are mine, and Christ can say in His turn: I am that sinner, that is to say, his sins, death, etc., are Mine, because he belongs to Me and I to him. For we through faith have been united into one flesh and bone." [23]

The Indwelling Christ

Christ dwells in believers through faith. For Luther, justification is not a naked imputation nor a simple declaration that the sinner is accounted righteous. Rather, a man is justified in, through, and because of a union with Christ that comes about by faith. Christ and the believer are united as Bridegroom and bride becoming "one flesh," [24] or "one cake." [25]

The believer does not live by his own spirit but by the Spirit of Christ, who dwells within him.[26] When a man comes to faith, the old Adam gets out and Christ enters, remains, and rules within his life; [27] and this is no wooden Christ but the risen, living Lord.[28]

Luther's classic statement is to be found in his larger commentary on Galatians: "Living in me as He does, Christ abolishes the Law, damns sin, and kills death; for at His presence all these cannot help disappearing. Christ is eternal Peace, Comfort, Righteousness, and Life. . . . Abiding and living in me, Christ removes and absorbs all the evils that torment and afflict me. This attachment to Him causes me to be liberated from the terror of the Law and of sin, pulled out of my own skin, and transferred into Christ. . . . Since I am in Him, no evil can harm me." [29]

It is his understanding of the indwelling Christ that made Luther take no credit for the spread of the Gospel throughout Europe. It was not his work that had created the many reforming movements. This was the work of Christ, not Luther, for only Christ can create Christians.

He wrote, "You do not believe because of men but because of the Word itself. There are many who believe because of me. However, only those are true Christians who would adhere to the Word even if they had heard that myself (God forbid) had denied and forsaken it. These are the ones who are not affected by whatever base, horrible, and shameful things they hear about me or about our assocuates,[30] for they believe not in Luther but in Christ Himself. . . . I myself do not know Luther either, nor do I want to know him, nor do I preach anything about him, but about Christ." [31]

Christ Is All in All

Christ is the summation of all justified sinners, for it is through His life they now live. In Christ each believer has become anonymous, because each now bears His name,[32] and there is no other name or authority that counts between God and man.

"Do not despair, therefore, but do this: pray with all your heart that the Lord Jesus may grant you to see that divine logic which teaches that Christ is other than Moses, pope, or all the world—indeed, that He is other and greater than our own conscience, which is above Moses and the pope. For if we must believe Moses and our conscience, which vexes us and convicts us by means of the Law, how much more must we believe Christ, the Lord of all things. . . . Though there be popes and councils without end, what are they compared with Christ? They are as a candle to the sun." [33]

"As the sun makes the day, so also does the radiance from Christ stream into all believing hearts and is at the same time in them all. As many eyes are see perfectly the rays of the sun, though there is only one sun, and as everyone has this ray perfectly, and all of them have it together, so it is also with Christ. We have Him altogether, and yet each has Him in his own heart. When He comes He lightens, rules us all through one faith. Then falsehood disappears, and the heart rightly sees God's Word and work. There is then a new world, a new people, and a new light." [34]

Summary of Luther's Faith and Doctrine

Martin Luther may not have compiled a theological textbook in which all the implications of his understanding of the doctrine of justification are neatly set out in an organized form, but he did produce what he called "my compendium of theology." It was a visual rather than a verbal compendium.

It was his official seal, which he designed to symbolize what was at the center of his theology, that is, the teaching that sinners are justified, forgiven through the grace of God, by faith alone in Jesus Christ. In a letter to his friend Lazarus Spengler he explained the meaning of this emblem:

"There is first to be a cross, black and placed in a heart, which should be in its natural color, so that I myself would be reminded that faith in the Crucified saves us. For if one believes from the heart, he will be justified. Even though it is a black cross, which mortifies and which also should hurt us, yet it leaves the heart in its natural color and does not ruin its nature; that is, the cross does not kill but keeps alive. For the just man lives by faith in the Crucified One.

"Such a heart is to be in the midst of a white rose, to symbolize that faith gives joy, comfort, and peace; in a word, it places the believer into a joyful white rose; for this faith does not give peace and joy as the world gives and, therefore, the rose is to be white and not red, for white is the color of spirits and of all the angels.

"Such a rose is to be in a sky-blue field, symbolizing that such joy in the Spirit and in faith is a beginning of the future heavenly joy; it is already a part of faith and is grasped through hope, even though not yet manifest.

"And around this field is a golden ring, symbolizing that in heaven such blessedness lasts forever and has no end, and in addition is precious beyond all joy and goods, just as gold is the most valuable and precious metal.

"May Christ, our dear Lord, be with your spirit until the life to come. Amen." [35]

64

ABBREVIATIONS

BC — *The Book of Concord,* ed. Theodore G. Tappert, Muhlenberg Press, Philadelphia, 1959.

CR — *Corpus Reformatorum,* ed. C. G. Bretschneider and H. E. Bindseil, Halle/Saale, 1834-60.

LCC — *The Library of Christian Classics,* published simultaneously in the United States and in Great Britain by the Westminster Press, Philadelphia, and the SCM Press, Ltd., London, 1953-.

LW — *Luther's Works,* American Edition. Fortress Press, Philadelphia, and Concordia Publishing House, St. Louis, 1955-.

StL — *D. Martin Luthers saemmtliche Schriften,* ed. J. G. Walch, 2nd edition. Concordia Publishing House, St. Louis, 1880-1910.

WA — *D. Martin Luthers Werke.* Kritische Gesamtausgabe, Weimar; Hermann Böhlau, 1883-.

NOTES

Chapter One

1. "For we hold that a man is justified by faith [alone] apart from works of law." (RSV)

2. LW, XXXV, 198.

3. WA, XXX/2, 657-76.

4. See LW, XXXIV, 337 (*Preface to the Complete Edition of Luther's Latin Writings,* 1545).

5. *Martin Luther* (London: Burns and Oates, 1964), p. 84.

6. For the views of Schmaus, who speaks from within Catholicism, and the Lutheran Rueckert, see Hans Küng, *Justification, the Doctrine of Karl Barth and a Catholic Reflection* (London: Burns and Oates, 1964), pp. 228 f., 208.

7. *The Structure of Lutheranism* (St. Louis: Concordia Publishing House, 1962), I, 79.

8. *Road to Reformation* (Philadelphia: Muhlenberg Press, 1946), pp. 128, 129-30, 141-42, 145, 148, 307, 334-35.

9. LW, XXXIV, 328 (*Preface to the Complete Editon of Luther's Latin Writings,* 1545).

10. "Therefore I lived as a monk, indeed not without sin but without reproach. For in the kingdom of the pope impiety and sacrilege pass for supreme piety; still less are they considered matters for reproach." LW, XLVIII, 333 ("Letter to Hans Luther," Nov. 21, 1521).

11. LW, XXXIV, 336-37. (*Preface to the Complete Edition of Luther's Latin Writings,* 1545).

12. *Luther's Progress to the Diet of Worms* (London: SCM Press Ltd., 1951), p. 39.

13. *Here I Stand* (New York: The New American Library, 1955), pp. 45-46.

14. Op. cit., pp. 87-117. See also Robert H. Fife, *The Revolt of Martin Luther* (New York: Macmillan and Co., 1957), pp. 197-202. It is interesting to note that 1513 is accepted by the Roman Catholic theologian Hans Küng, op. cit., p. 208.

15. *Luther Discovers the Gospel* (St. Louis: Concordia Publishing House, 1951), pp. 92-120. See also Otto W. Heick, "The Just Shall Live by Faith," *Concordia Theological Monthly*, XLIII (October 1971), 579-90.

16. Psalms 6, 32, 38, 51, 102, 130, 143. WA, I, 158-220. For the revised edition of 1525 see LW, XIV, 137-206.

17. E. g., on Ps. 143:11: "God's name is honored when men declare that He gives life and righteousness by grace without merit. The one can say: God is kind, gracious, merciful. These are His names that are to be praised. But the self-righteous honor their own names. They want to have life through their own righteousness. Therefore they despise the righteousness of God, which He grants the sinner by grace and by which He makes him alive in His freely given righteousness and in His truth." LW, XIV, 203.

18. LW, XXXI, 297-306.

19. Heinz Bluhm, "The Idea of Justice in Luther's First Publication," *Concordia Theological Monthly*, XXXVII (October 1966), 568.

20. Ibid., p. 565.

21. E. g., Tauler: ". . . they shall keep themselves from all the works of the flesh, which God hates, and shall have an earnest love to all righteousness, so that they are united with the bonds of their soul unto His divine nature. They shall, moreover, be ever striving to fulfill God's will, continually fixing their thoughts on Him, and keeping themselves from all that would be displeasing in His sight. . . ." *The History and Life of the Reverend Doctor John Tauler with Twenty-five of his Sermons*, trans. Susanna Winkworth (London: Smith, Elder, and Co., 1857), 264. For the influence of Tauler on Luther, see Steven E. Ozment, *Homo Spiritualis, a Comparative Study of the Anthropology of Joannes Tauler, Jean Gerson and Martin Luther (1509-16) in the Context of their Theological Thought* (Leiden: E. J. Brill, 1965), especially pp. 45-46, 197-209; and Bengt Hägglund, "The Background of Luther's Doctrine of Justification in Late Medieval Theology," *Lutheran World*, VIII, No. 1/2 (June 1961), 24-46.

22. Boehmer, p. 145.

23. Ibid., p. 148.

24. Reported in *Weekend Telegraph*, Dec. 16, 1966, No. 116, p. 31.

25. Op. cit., p. 307.

26. Apart from Boehmer's argument that Luther read into the German mystics

67

his doctrine of justification, we have Luther's significant letter to George Spenlein of April 8, 1516, in which his doctrine is well defined: "Now I should like to know whether your soul, tired of its own righteousness, is learning to be revived by and to trust in the righteousness of Christ. . . . Therefore, my dear Friar, learn Christ and Him crucified. Learn to praise Him, and, despairing of yourself, say, 'Lord Jesus, You are my righteousness, just as I am Your sin. You have taken upon Yourself what is mine and have given to me what is Yours. You have taken upon Yourself what You were not and have given to me what I was not.' Beware of aspiring to such purity that you will not wish to be looked upon as a sinner, or to be one. For Christ dwells only in sinners." LW, XLVIII, 12 f.

27. See Acts 16:30-31.

28. See Franz Lau, *Luther,* trans. Robert H. Fischer (London: SCM Press Ltd., 1963), pp. 81-85, and the second chapter of this present work.

29. LW, XLI, 111 *(On the Councils and the Church,* 1538). "Thereupon he [Martin Luther] spoke of his earliest books. He was now ashamed of them, he said, because in them he had conceded everything to the pope. 'Yes, I'd gladly have defended him because at that time I was like a drowning man, tossed about in the waves. Now [1539] I've fought my way through. I see that I tried to bring impossible contradictions into harmony. It was a wretched patchwork. The stitch wouldn't hold. I tried to sew the old on the new, and this caused a very bad rent." LW, LIV *(Table Talk),* No. 4462. (See Matt. 9:16.)

30. LCC, XVIII, 296-97. See also LW, XLIV, 36 f. *(Exhortation to All the Clergy Assembled in Augsburg,* 1530)

31. Luther's reply on being taken to task for using non-Scriptural terms in his *Theses Concerning Faith and Law* (1535), LW, XXXIV, 120 f.

Chapter Two

1. Boehmer, p. 179.

2. LW, XXXI, 17-33 (1517); Henry Bettenson, *Documents of the Christian Church* (London: Oxford University Press, 1963/2), 260-68. For a discussion of the significance and content of the 95 Theses, see Heinrich Bornkamm, *Luther's World of Thought* (St. Louis: Concordia Publishing House, 1958), pp. 36-54.

3. See *Summa Theologiae,* I-II, Qu. 113.

4. *Justification,* p. 118. "For the Catholic, the theology of justification is not suspended in mid-air but rather integrated into the all-encompassing mystery of the redemption of Jesus Christ and defined from this viewpoint." Ibid., p. 120.

5. See Paul Althaus, *Die Christliche Wahrheit. Lehrbuch der Dogmatik* (Gütersloh: Gerhard Mohr, 1952 ³), p. 236. Luther made the complaint against his opponents: "They have set faith not above but beside other virtues . . . although faith alone makes all other works good, acceptable, and worthy." LW, XLIV, 25 f. (*Treatise on Good Works*, 1520)

6. Luther called him "the Dresden dribbler" (LW, XXXV, 184), after he had stolen much of Luther's translation of the New Testament and called it his own.

7. StL, XVI, 1401, and CR, II, 299 (Letter dated Aug. 22, 1530).

8. StL, XVI, 1403 (Letter dated Aug. 26, 1530).

9. LW, XXXV, 181-202.

10. WA, XXX/2, 635-36.

11. See editorial comments WA, XXX/2, 627.

12. Heinz Bluhm, *Martin Luther, Creative Translator* (St. Louis: Concordia Publishing House, 1965), p. 125.

13. LW, XXXV, 188. (*On Translating: An Open Letter*, 1530)

14. Ibid., pp. 188-89.

15. "Is Christ's death and resurrection our work, that we do, or is it not? Of course it is not our work, nor the work of any law either. . . . What is the work by which we lay hold of Christ's death and resurrection? It cannot be any external work but only the external faith that is in the heart. Faith alone, indeed, all alone, without any works, lays hold of this death and resurrection when it is preached by the Gospel." Ibid., pp. 196-97.

16. Ibid., p. 195.

17. Ibid., p. 197.

18. *Die Reformation in Deutschland* (Freiburg: Herder and Co., 1949 ³) I, 292. See Bluhm, p. 131.

19. LW, XXXIV, 195 (*The Disputation Concerning Justification*, 1536).

20. LW, IV, 400 (*Lectures on Genesis*, 1535).

21. LW, XXIII, 109 (*Sermons on the Gospel of St. John*, 1530).

22. LW, XXIII, 207 (ibid.).

23. LW, XXXV. 363 (*Preface to the Acts of the Apostles*, 1533).

24. Ibid.

25. LW, XXVI, 3 (*Lectures on Galatians*, 1535).

26. LW, XXVI, 176 (ibid.).

27. StL, XIV, 168. (Luther's preface to Johannes Brenz' *Commentary on the Prophet Amos*, 1530)

28. Smalcald Articles (1536), Pt. II, Art. I; BC, 292.

29. Introductory essay in reprint of James Buchanan, *The Doctrine of Justification* (London: The Banner of Truth Trust, 1961), pp. 2-3.

30. LW, XIV, 197 (*The Seven Penitential Psalms*, 1525).

31. Smalcald Articles (1536), Pt. II, Art. I; BC, 292. See also LW, XII, 27 (*Commentary on Psalm 2*, 1532); LW, XXI, 59 (*Commentary on the Sermon on the Mount*, 1530); LW, XXII, 145 (*Sermons on the Gospel of St. John*, 1537); LW, XXVI, 9 (*Lectures on Galatians*, 1535); LW, LIV (*Table Talk*), No. 4422.

32. WA, XXXI, 255, quoted in the Formula of Concord (1577), S D, Art. III; BC, 540.

33. See LW, XXVII, 237 (*Lectures on Galatians*, 1519); LW, XLI, 237 (*Against Hanswurst*, 1541). It may well be that Luther received this idea from Tauler: "Dear children, be on your guard against this subtle self-seeking of nature, that ye do not fulfill good works of piety for the sake of earthly reward; for that has somewhat of the nature of simony, a sin which the holy church abhors above all others. . . . " Tauler, op. cit., p. 377.

34. LW, IV, 400 (*Lectures on Genesis*, 1535).

35. LW, XXVI, 395-96 (*Lectures on Galatians*, 1535). "The doctrine of faith and justification, or how we become righteous before God . . . drives out all false gods and idolatry; and when that is driven out, the foundation of the papacy falls, whereon it is built." *Tischreden*, quoted by Philip S. Watson, *Let God Be God, an Interpretation of the Theology of Martin Luther* (London: The Epworth Press, 1947), p. 4.

36. LW, XXVI, 176 (*Lectures on Galatians*, 1535).

37. Luther knew what it was to doubt: "A few times — when I did not bear this principal teaching in mind — the devil caught up with me and plagued me with Scripture passages until heaven and earth became too small for me. Then all the works and laws of man were right, and not an error was to be found in the whole papacy. In short, the only one who had ever erred was Luther. All my best works, teaching, sermons, and books had to be condemned." LW, XIV, 37 f. (*Commentary on Psalm 117*, 1530).

38. See LW, XXVI, 144 f. (*Lectures on Galatians*, 1535).

39. StL, VIII, 629-30 [see LW XXIV, 321 f.] (*Sermons on the Gospel of St. John*, 1538).

40. LW, XXVI, 283 (*Lectures on Galatians*, 1535). "For if we lose the doctrine of justification, we lose simply everything. Hence the most necessary and

important thing is that we teach and repeat this doctrine daily. . . . For it cannot be grasped or held enough or too much." LW, XXVI, 26. "It is very necessary, therefore, that this doctrine of faith be continually read and heard in public. . . . Therefore this doctrine can never be discussed or taught enough. If it is lost and perishes, the whole knowledge of truth, life, and salvation is lost and perishes at the same time. But if it flourishes, everything good flourishes — religion, true worship, the glory of God, and the right knowledge of all things and of all social conditions." LW, XXVI, 3. See LW, LIV *(Table Talk)*, No. 430.

"Neither can anyone teach correctly in the church or successfully resist any adversary if he does not maintain this article." StL, XIV, 168 (Luther's preface to Johannes Brenz' *Commentary on the Prophet Amos*, 1530). "As you have often heard, most excellent brothers, because that one article concerning justification even by itself creates true theologians, therefore, it is indispensable in the church and just as we must often recall it, so we must frequently work on it." LW, XXXIV, 157 *(The Disputation Concerning Justification*, 1536). "I do not know how I can change what I have heretofore constantly taught on this subject." Smalcald Articles, 1536, Pt. III, Art. XIII; BC, p. 315. See Ernst Walter Zeeden, *The Legacy of Luther* (London: Hollis and Carter, 1954), p. 6.

41. StL, XII, 494 f. (Sermon on Acts 10:34-43 for Easter Monday from Cruciger's *Sommerpostille*, 1544). "The fathers believed the same as we do. There is only one faith, even though it may have been less clear then; just as educated people now believe the same things as the uneducated, but more clearly." LW, XXV, 153 *(Lectures on Romans*, 1515-16, commenting on Rom. 1:17). See LW, XXVII, 241 *(Lectures on Galatians*, 1535): "For to believe in the forgiveness of sins through Christ is the highest article of our faith. And it is true that whoever believes this article has the forgiveness of sins." LW, XII, 27 *(Commentary on Psalm 2*, 1532).

42. "In short, whoever does not know the doctrine of justification takes away Christ the Propitiator." LW, XXVI, 28 *(Lectures on Galatians*, 1535).

43. LW, XXXIV, 91 *(Commentary of the Alleged Imperial Edict*, 1531).

Chapter Three

1. *Evangelical Theology: An Introduction* (London and Glasgow: Collins, The Fontana Library, 1965), pp. 97 f.

2. *Lectures on Justification* (London: J. G. F. and J. Rivington, 1840 [2], p. 372). See also pp. 15, 293, 381, 389, etc. Newman did not really understand Luther, and from the footnotes it seems that he knew only two of Luther's writings: *Commentary on Galatians* (1535) and *The Freedom of a Christian* (1520).

3. LW, XXXV, 370 *(Preface to the Epistle of St. Paul to the Romans*, 1522).

4. See LW, XXII, 334 (*Sermons on the Gospel of St. John*, 1537): "Faith is the engagement ring which betroths us to Christ."

5. Gustav Aulén, *Christus Victor, An Historical Study of the Three Main Types of the Atonement* (London: S.P.C.K., 1931), pp. 117-38, argues that Luther's theology of the atonement is of the "classic" type, that is, the drama of divine conflict and victory. Undoubtedly this is an element in Luther's theology, but it is not his complete view of the atonement, as Aulén would have us believe. For a critique of Aulén's position see John Warwick Montgomery's appendix in his translation *Chytraeus: On Sacrifice* (St. Louis: Concordia Publishing House, 1962), pp. 139-46, and Paul Althaus, *The Theology of Martin Luther* (Philadelphia: Fortress Press, 1966), pp. 218-23.

6. LW, XXXI, 351 f. (*The Freedom of a Christian*, 1520).

7. E. g., LW, XXI, 67 (*Commentary on the Sermon on the Mount*, 1530): "First we should constantly teach and emphasize faith, and then we should live according to faith. In this way everything we do will be done in faith and from faith, as I have always taught."

8. LW, XXXIV, 109-32.

9. LW, XXXIV, 109.

10. "Here Thomas [Aquinas] errs in common with his followers and Aristotle, who say, 'Practice makes perfect'; just as a harp player becomes a good harp player through long practice, so these fools think that the virtues of love, chastity, and humility can be achieved through practice." WA, X/3, 92 f. (sermon on John 20:19 ff., 1522).

11. LW, XXXIV, 113. "For it is true that both doubt and despair must follow when there is no faith in or knowledge of Christ." LW, XXIV, (*Sermons on the Gospel of St. John*, 1538). "Where there is no faith, there the kingdom of heaven also will remain outside; nor will spiritual poverty, meekness, and the like follow, but there will remain only scratching and scraping, quarrels and riots over temporal goods." LW, XXI, 15. (*Commentary on the Sermon on the Mount*, 1530)

12. *The Christian's Calling: Luther on Vocation*, trans. Carl C. Rasmussen (Edinburgh and London: Oliver and Boyd, 1958), pp. 237 f. "Unfaith denies that God is God." Althaus, p. 44.

13. WA, XVIII, 600-787; Martin Luther, *The Bondage of the Will* (hereafter B.O.W.), trans. and ed. J. I. Packer and O. R. Johnson (London: James Clarke and Co., 1957). See J. I. Packer, "Luther and Erasmus," *Concordia Theological Monthly*, XXXVII (April 1966), 207-21; Althaus, 156 f.; E. Gordon Rupp, *The Righteousness of God* (London: Hodder and Stoughton, 1953), pp. 270-85.

14. B.O.W., p. 162.

15. LW, **XXXV**, 371 (*Preface to the Epistle of St. Paul to the Romans,* 1522/46)

16. E. g., LW, **XXII**, 153 (*Commentary on the Sermon on the Mount,* 1530), 369, 474 (*Commentary on the Magnificat,* 1521); **XXIII**, 144 (*Sermons on the Gospel of St. John,* 1530); **XXVI**, 168 (*Lectures on Galatians,* 1535); **XXVII**, 28 (*Lectures on Galatians,* 1535).

17. LW, **XXXIV**, 109 f. (*Lectures on the Gospel of St. John,* 1537).

18. See 1 Cor. 1:23 and Gal. 3:13.

19. LW, **XXVI**, 269 (*Lectures on Galatians,* 1535). "Historical faith does not rely on the Word or trust in it. No, it says: 'I hear that Christ suffered and died, etc.' But true faith judges as follows: 'I believe that Christ suffered and died for me, etc.' About this I have no doubt, and in this faith I find rest. I trust in that word in opposition to sin and death." LW, **VIII**, 193 (*Lectures on Genesis,* 1535).

20. LW, **XXXIV**, 110 f. (*Sermons on the Gospel of St. John,* 1537).

21. LW, **XXI**, 309 (*Commentary on the Magnificat,* 1521). "A 'faith' that depends upon my apprehension of God's goodness in the shape either of my prosperous circumstances or of my peace of heart and mind, is simply not faith in *God.*" Watson, p. 43.

22. "For without faith God loses His glory, wisdom, righteousness, truthfulness, mercy, etc., in us; in short, God has none of His majesty or divinity where faith is absent. Nor does God require anything greater of man than that he attribute to Him His glory and His divinity; that is, that he regard Him not as an idol but as God." LW, **XXVI**, 227 (*Lectures on Galatians,* 1535).

23. Large Catechism, 1529, Pt. 1, BC, p. 365.

24. WA, **II**, 540 (sermon on John 10:12-16, 1523). "For it [faith] surely must not be such a sluggish, useless, deaf, or dead thing; it must be a living, productive tree which yields fruit. Therefore this is the rest, and this is the difference between faith which is genuine and faith that is false and colored: where faith is true, it manifests itself in life. A false faith, to be sure, bears the same name, employs the same words, and boasts of the same things, but nothing results from it." LW. **XXIV**, 265 (*Sermons on the Gospel of St. John,* 1537).

25. WA, **XXXVII**, 411. (Roland H. Bainton, *Luther's Meditations on the Gospels* [London: Lutterworth Press, 1963], p. 96.)

26. LW, **XXIII**, 23 (*Sermons on the Gospel of St. John,* 1530). See chapter 1, note 19.

27. LW, **XXXIV**, 109 (*Theses Concerning Faith and Law,* 1535).

28. Ibid., p. 110.

29. Ibid., p. 113.

30. LW, I, 9, on Gen. 1:2 (*Lectures on Genesis,* 1535).

31. "God enjoys bringing light out of darkness and making things out of nothing, etc. Thus He has created all things and thus He helps those who have been abandoned, He justifies sinners, He gives life to the dead, and saves the damned." WA, XL/3, 154 (*Commentary on the Psalms of Degrees,* 1532-33). "It is God's nature to make something out of nothing; hence one who is not yet nothing, out of him God cannot make anything." LW XIV, 163 (*The Seven Penitential Psalms,* 1525). See also LW, XLIII, 210 (*A Simple Way to Pray,* 1535).

32. LW, XXX, 14 (*Sermons on the First Epistle of St. Peter,* 1523).

33. LW, XXXVI, 301 (*The Adoration of the Sacrament,* 1523). "I believe that by my own reason or strength I cannot believe in Jesus Christ, my Lord, or come to Him. But the Holy Spirit has called me through the Gospel, enlightened me with His gifts, and sanctified and preserved me in true faith." Small Catechism, 1529, Pt. II, Art. 3, BC, 345.

34. LW, II, 266 f. (*Lectures on Genesis,* 1535).

35. LW, XXII, 285. (*Sermons on the Gospel of St. John,* 1538).

36. *Dr. Martin Luther's Saemmliche Werke* (First Elangen Edition), LVIII, 353, n. 7 *(Table Talk)*. See WA, Tr VI, No. 6727.

37. LW, XXXIV, 113 (*Theses Concerning Faith and Law,* 1535). See next chapter.

38. "For faith is not, as some of our moderns dream, a 'habitus,' quiet, snoring, and sleeping in the soul; but it is always turned towards God with a straight and perpetually looking and watching eye." WA, V, 460 (*Operationes in Psalmos,* 1518-21).

39. Elert, p. 152.

40. LW, I, 64 (*Lectures on Genesis,* 1535). See 2 Cor. 5:17.

41. LW, XXXVI, 40 (*The Babylonian Captivity of the Church,* 1520). Faith is "a living spiritual flame, by which hearts are set afire, born anew, and converted through the Holy Spirit." LW, XXXVI, 200 (*The Misuse of the Mass,* 1521). See John Wesley's account of his conversion: "In the evening I went very unwillingly to a society in Aldersgate Street, where one was reading Luther's Preface to the Epistle to the Romans. About a quarter before nine, while he was describing the change which God works in the heart through faith in Christ, I felt my heart strangely warmed. I felt I did trust Christ, Christ alone for salvation; and an assurance was given me that He had taken away my sins, even mine, and saved me from the law of sin and death." *Journal,* May 24, 1738.

42. "For faith is and must be a confidence of the heart which does not waver, reel, tremble, fidget, or doubt but remains constant and is sure of itself." LW, XV, 272 (*Treatise on the Last Words of David*, 1543).

43. "Justification is . . . only through faith . . . not piece by piece, but in one lump." StL, XII, 219 f. (Sermon on Gal. 4:1-7 for Sunday after Christmas, 1522).

44. LCC, XVIII, 196 (Letter to the Christians in Riga, etc., August 1523). For Luther's approach to the problem of what happens when death intervenes before faith, see his *Letter to Hans von Rechenberg* (1522?), LW, XLIII, 51-55.

45. LW, XXXIV, 110 (*Theses Concerning Faith and Law, 1535*).

46. Ibid.

47. Ibid., p. 111. On Gal. 2:20: "Therefore read these words *'me'* and *'for me'* with great emphasis, and accustom yourself to accepting this *'me'* with a sure faith and applying it to yourself. Do not doubt that you belong to the number of those who speak this *'me.'* Christ did not love only Peter and Paul and give Himself for them, but the same grace belongs and comes to us as to them; therefore we are included in this *'me'*." LW, XXVI, 179 (*Lectures on Galatians, 1535*). "These words, OUR, US, FOR US, must be written in letters of gold. He who does not believe this is not a Christian." LW, XVII, 221 (*Lectures on Isaiah, 1527-30*).

48. Op. cit., p. 50.

49. Jaroslav Pelikan, *Luther the Expositor* (St. Louis: Concordia Publishing House, 1959), p. 48.

50. See Heinrich Bornkamm, *Das Wort Gottes bei Luther* (Munich: Charles Kaiser Verlag, 1933); Lennart Pinomaa, *Faith Victorious: An Introduction to Luther's Theology* (Philadelphia: Fortress Press, 1963), pp. 101-10; Pelikan, pp. 48-70; Althaus, pp. 35-52; Watson, pp. 149-89; Herman Sasse, "Luther and the Word of God," *Accents in Luther's Theology: Essays in Commemoration of the 450th Anniversary of the Reformation*, ed. Heino O. Kadai (St. Louis and London: Concordia Publishing House, 1967), pp. 47-97.

51. LW, XXII, 8-9 on John 1:1 (*Sermons on the Gospel of St. John*, 1537).

52. LW, XXXVI, 42 (*The Babylonian Captivity of the Church*, 1520). "Faith, moreover, comes only through God's Word or Gospel, which preaches Christ, saying that He is God's Son and a man, and has died and risen again for our sakes," LW, XXXV, 368 (*Preface to the Epistle of St. Paul to the Romans*, 1522/46).

53. LW, XXXVI, 169 (*The Misuse of the Mass*, 1521).

54. LW, LI, 76 (*Eight Sermons at Wittenberg*, 1522). "Faith does not follow

the dictates of reason and the senses but stands by calmly and permits God to take the lead." LW, XIII, 5 f. (*Commentary on Psalm 68*, 1521).

55. LW, XXX, 296 (*Sermons on the First Epistle of St. John*, 1527).

56. LW, XXIII, 76 (*Sermons on the Gospel of St. John*, 1530). "Wherever there is faith, eternal life has already begun." LW, XIV, 88 (*Commentary on Psalm 118*, 1530). See LW, XXI, 306 f. (*Commentary on the Magnificat*, 1521).

57. WA, X/3, 239 (Sermon on Matt. 20:20-28, 1522).

58. See chapter 5.

59. LW, XXXIV, 111 (*Theses Concerning Faith and Law*, 1535). See LW, XXXV, 89 (*A Treatise on the New Testament, That Is, the Holy Mass*, 1520), and chapter 4.

60. LW, XIII, 243 (*Commentary on Psalm 110*, 1535).

61. LW, XXII, 268 (*Sermons on the Gospel of St. John*, 1537).

62. StL, IX, 9 (*Lectures on Galatians*, 1535). See LW, XXIV, 48, 52 (*Sermons on the Gospel of St. John*, 1537).

63. LW, XXX, 287 (*Sermons on the First Epistle of St. John*, 1527).

64. LW, XXIV, 42, on John 14:6 (*Sermons on the Gospel of St. John*, 1537). See LW, XXVII, 171 f. (*Lectures on Galatians*, 1519).

65. LW, XXIII, 28 (*Sermons on the Gospel of St. John*, 1530). See LW, XXX, 42 f. (*Sermons on the First Epistle of St. Peter*, 1523). "You should under no circumstances allow yourself to become impatient because you do not at once have strong faith. St. Paul declares in Rom. ch. 14 [:1] and 15 [:1] that those who are weak in the faith are not cast off. God is not that kind of father who casts off sick and erring children; if He were, He would have no children." LCC, XVIII, 121 (Letter to Valentine Hausemann, June 24, 1532).

66. LW, XXXIV, 114.

67. LW, XXVI, 227 (*Lectures on Galatians*, 1535). See also LW, XIV, 81 (*Commentary on Psalm 118*, 1530). "Suppose it were true that our sins were forgiven because of our contrition . . . and not because of God's Word alone. . . . If this were so, a man could boast before God that he had attained grace and forgiveness by his own contrition and merit and not solely by the mercy of God." LW, XXXII, 47 (*Defense and Explanation of All the Articles*, 1521).

68. See Thomas Aquinas, *Summa Theologica*, I-II, Q. III, Art. 1.

69. LW, XXVI, 129 f. (*Lectures on Galatians*, 1535). "You must prove your name as a Christian by faith and nothing else, that is, so as to believe that

Christ's righteousness is yours, that His life, death, and everything that Christ is, is yours, given to you." LW, LI, 112 (Sermon on Matt. 22:37-39, 1522).

70. Op. cit., pp. 98 f.

Chapter Four

1. Arthur Carl Piepkorn, in a review of Ragnar Bring, *Das Verhaeltnis von Glauben und Werken in der Lutherischen Theologie* (Munich: Chr. Kaiser Verlag, 1955), *Concordia Theological Monthly*, XXXVIII (April 1967), 278.

2. See G. Friedrich Bente, *Historical Introductions to the Book of Concord* (St. Louis: Concordia Publishing House, 1965), pp. 112-24.

3. Ibid., p. 115.

4. Ibid., p. 122.

5. Quoted by Cecil Headlam, *The Story of Nuremberg* (London: J. M. Dent and Co., 1899), p. 82.

6. James Anthony Froude, *Life and Letters of Erasmus* (London: Longmans, Green and Co., 1916), p. 344.

7. LW, XLIV, 24 (*Treatise on Good Works*, 1520). "Therefore, when some people say, as they do, that when we preach faith alone, good works are forbidden, it is as if I were to say to a sick man, 'If you had health, you would have full use of your limbs, but without health the works of all your limbs are nothing,' and from this he wanted to infer that I had forbidden the works of his limbs." LW, XLIV, 34 (*Treatise on Good Works*, 1520).

8. An English translation is given as Appendix I in Henry Eyster Jacobs, *Martin Luther: The Hero of the Reformation*, 1483-1546 (New York and London: G. P. Putnam's Sons, 1898), pp. 413-35.

9. Ibid., p. 421.

10. Ibid. The Council of Trent later endorsed the pope's condemnation, Sess. VI, can. 25: "If anyone saith that, in every good work, the just sins venially at least, or—which is still more intolerable—mortally, and consequently deserves eternal punishments . . . let him be anathema."

11. WA, II, 416.

12. LW, XXXII, 7-99.

13. See Matt. 7:26—a recurring image in Luther's *Treatise on Good Works* (1520).

14. LW, XXXII, 83-86 (*Defense and Explanation of All the Articles*, 1521).

15. Ibid., 19-29.

16. LW, XXXII, 84 (*Defense and Explanations of All the Articles*, 1521). See Luther's letter to George Spalatin, April 13, 1520, LW, XLVIII, 156-59.

17. LW, XXXI, 40 (*Heidelberg Disputation*, 1518). "Although the works of man always seem attractive and good, they are nevertheless likely to be mortal sins." LW, XXXI, 39.

18. LW, XXXI, 46. (It is evident that at this early stage—the *Heidelberg Disputation* of 1518—of his reforming career, when Luther speaks of fear, he is speaking of what he later came to call faith.) "Nor does speaking in this manner give cause for despair, but for arousing the desire to humble one's self and seek the grace of Christ. It is certain that man must utterly despair of his own ability before he is prepared to accept Christ." LW, XXXI, 40.

19. LW, XII, 348 (*Commentary on Psalm 51*, 1538). "This hereditary sin is so deep a corruption of nature that reason cannot understand it. It must be believed because of the revelation in the Scriptures." Smalcald Articles, 1536, Pt. III, Art. I, BC, 302. "Original sin . . . [is] . . . not merely a lack, deficiency, or want, but sin of such sort that it condemns and separates from God all men descended from Adam. . . . As now, therefore, all men are sinners subject to sin and death, and moreover to the devil likewise, it is impossible for any man by his own exertions and good works to rid, dis-embarrass, and free himself from them by these works, or by their means justify himself anew, or become assuredly good and just; nor can he prepare or dispose himself for justice or justification; nay, the more he proposes, or intends, laboring of himself to exonerate, free, or purge and justify himself, the worse does his position become." Schwabach Articles, 1529, Arts. IV and V, Jacobs, pp. 438-39.

20. "For so long as man does what is within his power, he is smug." LW, XXVII, 292 (*Lectures on Galatians*, 1519).

21. LW, XXVI, 397 (*Lectures on Galatians*, 1535).

22. *The Essential Erasmus*, trans. and ed. John P. Dolan (New York and London: The New American Library, 1964), pp. 226-70.

23. Ibid., p. 258.

24. Ibid., p. 259.

25. Ibid., p. 263.

26. Ibid., p. 265.

27. Ibid., p. 266.

28. Ibid., p. 267.

29. Ibid., p. 270.

30. LW, XXVI, 396 (*Lectures on Galatians, 1535*). See LW, XXVI, 9, and LW, LIV (*Table Talk*), No. 1319.

31. "Sin is a heavy and grievous and terrifying burden; yet it cannot be taken away through outward works of man, but only through the inner work of God." LW, XIV, 171 (*Commentary on Psalm 147, 1532*). Luther sees sin essentially as an internal problem, but for Erasmus it is an external problem. The latter says: "It is a sin to think of evil, but it is even worse to try to accomplish what you have thought." Op. cit., p. 261. Thus Erasmus reverses the meaning of Jesus in Matt. 5:21-48, where the Lord stresses the interior nature of sin.

    For the debate between Luther and Erasmus see *Luther and Erasmus: Free Will and Salvation*, ed. E. Gordon Rupp et al., LCC, XVII (Philadelphia: The Westminster Press, 1969). Later in life Luther summarized his opinion of Erasmus as follows: "Every time Erasmus, a marvelously learned and eloquent man, begins to speak about justification and matters of faith he stammers most wretchedly and talks like a fool." LW, II, 67 (*Lectures on Genesis, 1535*).

32. "It is God's nature to make something out of nothing; hence one who is not yet nothing, out of him God cannot make anything. . . . Therefore no proud saint, no wise or righteous person can become God's material, and God's purpose cannot be fulfilled in him. He remains in his own work and makes a fictitious, pretended, false saint of himself, that is, a hypocrite." LW, XIV, 163 (*Commentary on Psalm 147, 1532*). "Now with us the situation is that Adam must get out and Christ come in, Adam become as nothing, and Christ alone remain and rule. . . . For the old Adam, with which we were born, makes sinful and nullifies also the good works." LW, XIV, 167. See also p. 169 (*Commentary on Psalm 147, 1532*).

33. "If only they pray, fast, establish endowments, go to confession, and do enough is supposed to be all right, although in all this they have had no faith in the grace of God and no certainty of His approval. In fact, they regard these works most highly when they have done a great many major ones for a long time, without any such confidence, and they look for good only after the works have been performed. And so they build their confidence not on God's favor but on the works they have done." LW, XLIV, 29 (*Treatise on Good Works, 1520*).

34. LW, XLIV, 64.

35. LW, XXXI, 363 (*The Freedom of a Christian, 1520*).

36. Works are "inanimate things," LW, XXXI, 353 (*The Freedom of a Christian, 1520*), and are "not good in themselves." LW, XLIV, 54 (*Treatise on Good Works, 1520*).

37. "Since faith alone justifies, it is clear that the inner man cannot be justified,

freed, or saved by any outer work or action at all, and that these works, whatever their character, have nothing to do with the inner man. . . . Wherefore it ought to be the first concern of every Christian to lay aside all confidence in works and increasingly to strengthen faith alone and through faith to grow in knowledge, not of works, but of Jesus Christ, who suffered and rose for him." LW, XXXI, 347 (*The Freedom of a Christian*, 1520).

38. "After Christ, therefore, the works of the Law are like riches, honor, civic righteousness, and any other temporal thing. If you have them, you are not on this account better in the sight of God; if you lack them, you are not on this account worse." LW, XXVII, 203 (*Lectures on Galatians*, 1519).

39. "But you would be very wicked if you were to assert that you must have them [i. e., good works] in order to please God." (Ibid.)

40. "Works, being inanimate things, cannot glorify God, although they can, if faith is present, be done *to* the glory of God. Here, however, we are not inquiring what works and what kind of works are done but who it is who does them, who glorifies God and brings forth the works. This is done by faith which dwells in the heart and is the source and substance of all our righteousness." LW, XXXI, 353 (*The Freedom of a Christian*, 1520).

41. LW, XLIV, 26 (*Treatise on Good Works*, 1520).

42. LW, XXIII, 112 (*Sermons on the Gospel of St. John*, 1530). "No one is righteous before faith . . . the righteous man lives through faith in the sight of God, which means that faith is a man's righteousness, life, and salvation in the sight of God, and that righteousness does not come before faith, but that righteousness and faith come through faith." LW, XXVII, 259 (*Lectures on Galatians*, 1519). See LW, XXIII, 58 and 106 (*Sermons on the Gospel of St. John*, 1530); LW, LI, 63 (Sermon on John 20:19-20, 1521).

43. LW, XXXI, 347 (*The Freedom of a Christian*, 1520).

44. "A human being, rather than his works, must be just, and that he is accepted by God without any works, solely through grace, which faith believes and apprehends." LW, I, 259 (*Lectures on Genesis*, 1535).

45. LW, XXXI, 361 (*The Freedom of a Christian*, 1520).

46. LW, XXVI, 6 (*Lectures on Galatians*, 1535)

47. LW, XLIV, 23, 25, and 60 (*Treatise on Good Works*, 1520). Luther later clarified this confusion. In the *Disputation Concerning Justification* (1536) he said: "Although our calling faith a work can be tolerated, nevertheless, those words should be avoided altogether. . . . Faith is indeed called a work in its place, but we ought to avoid it. . . . That I love God is the work of God alone. Although that I believe is also a work, still it should not be spoken of as a work. We ought to let every word remain in its own category so that the question is not thrown into a complete jumble." LW, XXXIV, 159 f. See

LW, LIV *(Table Talk)*, No. 4655; LW, XXX, 14 f. *(Sermons on the First Epistle of St. Peter*, 1523).

48. LW, XLIV, 40 *(Treatise on Good Works*, 1520). "Compared with this work [of faith] the other good works are like the other commandments would be if they were without the first and as if there were no God." Ibid., 30. "Nor does faith, as a work, make just; but it makes just because it apprehends the mercy which is offered in Christ." LW, I, 259 *(Lectures on Genesis*, 1535).

49. LW, XLIV, 38 f. *(Treatise on Good Works*, 1520). "For faith is a divine work which God demands of us; but at the same time He Himself must implant it in us, for we cannot believe by ourselves." LW, XXIII, 23 *(Sermons on the Gospel of St. John*, 1530).

50. LW, XLIV, 34 *(Treatise on Good Works*, 1520).

51. Ibid., 113.

52. LW, XXXI, 349 *(The Freedom of a Christian*, 1520).

53. E. Theodore Bachman, in a footnote to a passage in *On Translating: An Open Letter*. LW, XXXV, 196, n. 63.

54. James 2:26. On the Epistle of James Luther writes: "I praise it and consider it a good book, because it sets up no doctrines of men but vigorously promulgates the law of God." LW, XXXV, 395 *(Preface to the Epistle of St. James*, 1522).

55. LW, XXXIV, 111 *(Theses Concerning Faith and Law*, 1535). "Where faith is of the right kind, there deeds also follow; and the greater the faith, the greater the deeds. Faith of the right kind is indeed something powerful, mighty, and active. To it nothing is impossible; nor does it take a rest or take a holiday." WA, X/1, 1, 269 (sermon for St. Stephen's Day on Acts 6:8-14, *Weinachtspostille*, 1522).

56. LW, XLIV, 27 *(Treatise on Good Works*, 1520). See LW, XXXV, 361. *(Preface to the New Testament*, 1522)

57. E. g., LW, XXI, 61, 149 f. *(Commentary on the Sermon on the Mount*, 1530); LW, XXVII, 330 *(Lectures on Galatians*, 1519); LW, XXXI, 361 *(The Freedom of a Christian*, 1520); LW, XLIV, 25, 79, 98, 109 *(Treatise on Good Works*, 1520).

58. LW, XXXI, 360 *(The Freedom of a Christian*, 1520). See LW, XLVIII, 25.

59. LW, XXII, 279-81 *(Sermons on the Gospel of St. John*, 1538).

60. See LW, IV, 174 *(Lectures on Genesis*, 1535). "To trust in works is to become incurable hypocrites." LW, XXVII, 172 *(Lectures on Galatians*, 1519).

61. LW, XXXV, 371 *(Preface to the Epistle of St. Paul to the Romans*, 1522).

"Let our own good works be idle, and let God work in us." LW, XLIV, 77 (*Treatise on Good Works*, 1520). See LW, XIV, 171 (*The Seven Penitential Psalms*, 1525).

62. LW, XXVII, 168 f. See also p. 174 (*Lectures on Galatians*, 1519).

63. LW, XXXV, 197 (*On Translating: An Open Letter*, 1530). "The performance of many works . . . [is] . . . the monstrous theology which has Aristotle as its head and Christ as its feet . . . as if it were not enough to believe in Christ, in whom our righteousness, redemption, satisfaction, life and glory are by faith alone." LW, XXVII, 328. See also p. 332 (*Lectures on Galatians*, 1519).

64. LW, LIV (*Table Talk*), No. 327. See also No. 388.

Chapter Five

1. *Tischreden oder Colloquia Doct. Mart. Luthers . . . Nach den Heubstuecken unserer Christlichen Lere, zusammen getragen* (Tabletalk or Sayings of Dr. Martin Luther . . . collected together under the chief articles of our Christian Doctrine), ed. Johann Aurifaber, Eisleben, 1566. That Aurifaber intended this volume as a systematic presentation of Luther's theology, rather than as a simple collection of his table conversations, is demonstrated by his use of other material from Luther's letters, sermons, and printed works.

2. For example, his proposed treatises on *Justification* (WA, XXX/2, 657-76) and *Music* (WA, XXX/2, 695-6).

3. LW, XXXIII, 16 (*The Bondage of the Will*, 1526). See also LW, XLVIII, 297 (Letter to Melanchthon, Sept. 9, 1521).

4. LW, LIV (*Table Talk*), No. 5511.

5. *Melanchthon and Bucer* (LCC, XIX), ed. Wilhelm Pauck (Philadelphia: The Westminster Press, 1969), pp. 88 f. (Italics added.) Compare the Fourth Article of the Augsburg Confession, BC, p. 30, and the address of Luther's letter to Melanchthon of June 27, 1530: "To Philip Melanchthon, beloved disciple of Christ and bearer of Christ: grace and peace in Christ—in Christ, I say, and not in the world. Amen." LCC, XVIII, 146.

6. WA, X/1, 1, 468 (*Church Postil*, Epistle for New Year's Day, 1522). "Christ is God's grace, mercy, righteousness, truth, wisdom, power, comfort, and salvation, given to us by God without any merit on our part. Christ, I say, not as some express it in blind words 'causally,' that He grants righteousness and remains absent Himself, for that would be dead. Yes, it is not given at all unless Christ Himself is present, just as the radiance of the sun and the heat of the fire are not present if there is no sun and no fire." LW, XIV, 204 (*The Seven Penitential Psalms*, 1525). See also LW, XXXVI, 344 (*The Sacrament of the Body and Blood of Christ—Against the Fanatics*, 1526).

7. LW, XXIV, 25 (*Sermons on the Gospel of St. John*, 1537-8). See also LW,

XXIII, 61 (*Sermons on the Gospel of St. John*, 1531); LW, XXXIV, 27 (*Exhortation to all Clergy Assembled in Augsburg*, 1530).

8. "I say that, if we are ever to stand before God with a right and uncolored faith, we must come to the point where we learn clearly to distinguish and separate between ourselves, our life, and Christ the mercy-seat. He who will not do this, but immediately runs headlong to the judgment seat, will find it all right and get a good knock on the head. . . . I know of no other comfort, help, or counsel for my salvation except that Christ is my mercy-seat, who did no sin or evil and both died and rose again for me and sits at the right hand of the Father and takes me to Himself. . . . Thus faith remains pure and unalloyed, because then it makes no pretensions and seeks no glory or comfort save in the Lord Christ alone. The man who can do this will be the justified man." LW, LI, 282 f. (*Sermon on the Sum of the Christian Life*, 1532); "Christ is the cause of our justification." LW, XXXIV, 192 (*Disputation Concerning Justification*, 1536).

9. BC, 365 (Large Catechism, 1529).

10. LW, XXIII, 129 (*Sermons on the Gospel of St. John*, 1531); "If the article on justification hadn't fallen, the brotherhoods, pilgrimages, masses, invocation of saints, etc., would have found no place in the church. If it falls again (which may God prevent!), these idols will return." LW, LIV (*Table Talk*), No. 4422; "One shouldn't think of any other God than Christ; whoever doesn't speak through the mouth of Christ is not God. God wants to be heard through the Propitiator, so He'll listen to nobody except through Christ." LW, LIV (*Table Talk*), No. 1543.

11. LW, XLIV, 298 f. (*The Judgment of Martin Luther on Monastic Vows*, 1521).

12. LW, XXVII, 173 (*Lectures on Galatians*, 1519).

13. LW, XXIV, 52 (*Sermons on the Gospel of St. John*, 1537-8).

14. LW, XLIV, 254 (*The Judgment of Martin Luther on Monastic Vows*, 1521).

15. LW, XLIII, 54 f. (*Letter to Hans von Rechenberg*, 1522).

16. LW, XXIV, 48 (*Sermons on the Gospel of St. John*, 1537-8).

17. Ibid., p. 366. See also LW, LIV (*Table Talk*), No. 4331.

18. LW, XXX, 12 (*Sermons on the First Epistle of St. Peter*, 1522).

19. LW, XIV, 170 (*The Seven Penitential Psalms*, 1525).

20. LW, XLVIII, 12 (*Letter to George Spenlein*, April 8, 1516).

21. LW, XXVII, 241 (*Lecture on Galatians*, 1519).

22. LW, LI, 63 (Sermon preached at Erfurt, April 7, 1521). See also LW, XXI, 60 (*Commentary on the Sermon on the Mount*, 1530-32); LW, XXIV,

346 f. (*Sermons on the Gospel of St. John*, 1537-8); LW, XXVII, 168, 222, 240, etc. (*Lectures on Galatians*, 1519); and chapter 3 above.

23. WA, V, 311 (*Commentary on the First Twenty-Two Psalms*, 1518-22), quoted by Willem J. Kooiman, *Luther and the Bible* (Philadelphia: Muhlenberg Press, 1961), p. 51.

24. LW, XXXI, 351 (*The Freedom of a Christian*, 1520).

25. WA, XXVIII, 188 (Sermon on John 17:22 f., Oct. 24, 1528).

26. LW, XXVII, 238 (*Lectures on Galatians*, 1519). See also LW, XII, 331 (*Commentary on Psalm 51*, 1538).

27. LW, XIV, 167 (*The Seven Penitential Psalms*, 1525). See also LW, XXVII, 289, 332 (*Lectures on Galatians*, 1519).

28. LW, XLIII, 65 (*Letter of Consolation to All Who Suffer Persecution*, 1522).

29. LW, XXVI, 167 (*Lectures on Galatians*, 1535).

30. Luther is referring her to the many false rumors that were circulated about him.

31. LW, XLIII, 68 (*Letter of Consolation to All Who Suffer Persecution*, 1522). "I dare not boast of converting people, but I must ascribe all this to the Lord Christ." LW, XXX, 21 (*Sermons on the First Epistle of St. Peter*, 1522).

32. LW, XXVII, 280 (*Lectures on Galatians*, 1519).

33. LCC, XVIII, 123 (*Letter to Gregory Rosseken*, March 28, 1533).

34. WA, IX, 669 (Sermon on Luke 24:13 f., April 1, 1521), trans. Roland H. Bainton, *Luther's Meditations on the Gospels* (London: Lutterworth Press, 1963), p. 150.

35. LW, XLIX, 358 f. (Letter, July 8, 1530).